THE SECRET AMERICAN BOMBER GIRLS

BY

BILL MUNTEAN

PUBLISHED BY DAUGHTERS
PRESS,USA
COPYRIGHT©2018

To my fried Lynn
"Fly High"
Bill Muntean

This book is dedicated to the millions of women who served during WW II while in the:

Finland Lotta Svärd
Finland Lotta Svärd anti-aircraft guns
Romanian White Squadron (air ambulance)
Canadian WAVS, WAAF, WRENS
India's WACS
French Resistance
Polish Resistance
Italian Partisans
Partisans
German anti aircraft spotters
German Luftnachrichten-helferinnen
Soviet snipers, anti aircraft personal, drench fighters and aviators
The Red Cross
The Code Breakers
The Spies
British AFS
British RAF WRENS
British ATS
British ATA
Yugoslavian Partisans
The Under Estimated
Army and Navy Nurse Corp
American USO
American WAC
American WAVES
American WASP
American SPARS
American Marines Res.
The Secret American Bomber Girls

I would like to acknowledge:

Editor: Christina Sheridan
Illustrator: Stephanie Richoll
Munitions Advisor: Ron Spano

This story is true, ripped from recently declassified top secret papers of the United States Army Air Force. The author attempts to explain his sources and then fills in the missing facts based on historic events. Any similarity and likeness to anyone living or dead is purely coincidental.

The author has opted to hang a few rules of grammar to make his book look and flow better. Iffen anyone has a problem with that, they can take it to the Chaplain.

CHAPTER 1

THE FLIGHT OF 'THE ANGRY ALBATROSS'

"Lieutenant White, check on the starboard waist gunner. I think she's been hit!" ordered the war bird's pilot who kinked her neck to the right so to speak with the navigator/radio operator seated behind the co-pilot of a North American B-25 Mitchell medium bomber named 'The Angry Albatross'. The plane had a picture of an albatross with an angry expression across its beak and eagle talons in place of webbed feet painted on its nose. The pilot, Captain Jennifer Edwards, was a pretty 26 year old, making her older than most ladies in the Army Air Corp. She was plain looking, tall and thin, blue eyed with long brown locks that poured out from under her captain's cap. She had to shout to be heard above the roar of the plane's twin 1700 rpm Wright R-2600 engines. After hearing moaning over the intercom, she was mentally able to track it back to her waist gunner. One has to know these things to be a Captain of an American warplane.

"Right Captain," responded Lieutenant Virginia White, the navigator/radio operator on board the plane. Unbeknownst to the United States Army Air Force (the USAAF), Virginia, who was 5' 5" tall, skinny, with short blonde hair, tanned olive skin, blue eyes, a broad face and pudgy checks, was only 16 years old.

Accompanying Virginia on the aircraft was the pilot, co-pilot, two waist gunners, a top turret gunner, a tail gunner and a bombardier. Her flight of 36 bombers was roaring through the clear blue sky over Germany in August of 1943 flying toward their target, the heavily protected ball bearing plant at Schweinfurt, about 100 miles west of Frankfurt. A British bomber squadron had hit the plant the night before. An American aerial armada assaulted the bearing plant that morning. The women's job was to be sure the plant could not be rebuilt.

The mission was on time, on course and going well until the Mitchells were jumped by a squadron of German Focke 190 fighter planes that attacked from out of the sun. The German pilots opened up on the B-25s. Each fighter plane was well armed. Virginia's plane took a few hits as the Germans made their first pass. She looked from her window to see a B-25 on fire, spiraling toward Earth.

"C'mon girls, bail out!" said Lt. Honey Blake, the co-pilot watching the burning war bird plummet. "Count the chutes everyone."

"I see two," reported Lt. Marie Trembley from the nose.

"And three more," announced Lt. Blake.

"I see five all together," reported Lt. Joanna Owens, the tail gunner. There were five women bailing out of the burning plane meaning three would surely die when the plane impacted the Earth.

Virginia needed to tend to the injured starboard waist gunner so with first aid kit in hand she quickly crawled on all fours through a short tunnel over the bomb bay that held the bomber's cargo of 300 pound bombs, to the waist gunners. Virginia sat on the floor of the cramped space next to Julie, the gunner. Julie had caught a piece of shrapnel from a bullet fired by the Fw-190. The hot metal passed through the plane's thin aluminum external skin before slicing through Julie's side. She was parked on her butt with her back against the plane's bulkhead and her bloody hands pressed against the wound quietly moaning.

"You're gonna be alright," said Virginia, not really knowing how badly the gunner was cut. It was just something people say in situations such as that one. Fortunately, the hot shrapnel cauterized the veins and the capillaries in the wound so Virginia was able to staunch the bleeding with a simple gauze pressure bandage. "What are you doing!!?" she demanded of the gunner who was struggling to her feet. "You are hurt and need to lay flat until we get back to base."

"Nothin' doin'. Help me back to my feet. I got work that needs to be done," said Julie.

"Julie, be sensible. If you start bleeding again, I may not be able to stop it. Stay down."

"That's what you New York Yankees do, but us Florida girls live to fight."

"I'm an Indians fan from Ohio."

"Just help me to my gun, Gini."

Virginia chose not to argue and assisted the thin 5' 4" 19 year old to her 30 caliber machine gun. She was done tending to Julie so once again Virginia slipped back through the tunnel and found the way back to her post behind the co-pilot's seat.

Just then, another group of Fw-190 closed in on the B-25s. Julie pulled back the bolt on her 30 cal. cocking her machine gun before getting a bead on one of the incoming attackers. "C'mon, just a little to the left," said

Julie before letting loose a barrage of bullets. The Focke instantly became a cloud of smoke when Julie's shells nested into the enemy fighter's gas tank. "Yes, how do you like that?" Julie shouted from her open window.

"Look out ladies, flak ahead...like I didn't see that comin'," reported Captain Edwards.

"Can we climb above it, Capt.?" inquired Lt. Blake.

"No, that will throw us off target."

The flak...bursts of anti-aircraft fire...darkened the sky around the small bombers. Virginia felt the plane bounce when a shell exploded near a wing. A hot shard of shrapnel pierced the plane's paper thin outer skin landing on the navigator's table top igniting her charts on fire. Virginia calmly snuffed out the flames without incident. A second American aircraft reported the loss of their port engine and planned an emergency landing.

Virginia quickly did the math calculating their position. "Pilot from Navigator, target in two minutes," she reported over the intercom.

"Bombardier from Pilot, you have the plane."

Lt. Marie Trembley's small five foot frame was crouched down in the Plexiglas bubble in the front of the aircraft. Hunched over the bomb site, she watched through the eyepiece as the target came into view. She was in control of the plane calculating air speed and wind direction. The Germans tried to mask her view of the target with a smoke screen but it was too little too late. "40 seconds to target," Marie reported before she shook her head tossing her long black hair out of her face. She looked through the eye piece of the bomb site.

After what seemed like an eternity of continually being bounced around by exploding flak, Marie reported 20 seconds. When the lady was sure the plane was properly positioned, her thumb pressed the button that released the plane's deadly payload. "Bombs away!!" she shouted into her intercom. The crew felt the bomber lurch becoming 3600 pounds lighter.

"Right on target," reported Joanna the tail gunner, "Look at that baby burn. We should have brought some weenies and marshmallows."

"Those would be the only weenies on the plane," said Teresa the port waist gunner.

"Or in the whole squadron," commented Honey, the co-pilot.

"Bandits, bandits 12 o'clock high," reported Lt. Sandy O'Malley, the top turret gunner. "There's a shit load of 'em!"

Jennifer pulled back on the yoke and stepped on the gas in an attempt to escape the oncoming speedy Fw-190's. The German planes in the distance began to sparkle meaning that they were shooting, trying to kill the crew of 'The Albatross'. Their shells slammed into the starboard side of the Mitchell. The plane rolled 20 degrees to port pitching Virginia head first into the metal box that surrounded the bomb bay. She fell to the floor of the plane and did not get up.

After being rendered unconscious for a few minutes, Virginia woke and struggled to her feet. She saw stars and heard ringing in her ears drowning out the constant thundering of the engines, but only for a moment or two. The intercom was all a jumbled with Jennifer shouting commands. Her head was still cloudy from the fall and blood gushed from a gash above her left eye blurring her vision. The American Bomber Girl found her med kit and proceeded to patch the bleeding hole above her eye.

Virginia had much to do and little time to do it in for the Germans were coming around to initiate another attack. "Virginia, I've been hit," reported the port gunner Lt. Teresa Gallo.

"And so has Sandy," announce Honey.

"I'm coming," said Virginia, grabbing an unconscious Sandy from the top turret and flopping her onto the floor of the aircraft. She too had a gouge in her head from shards of shrapnel from a shell that disengaged as it passed through the Plexiglas bubble that protected Sandy from the elements. She was unconscious but still breathing so she could wait. Virginia made her way to Teresa who had a whole in her abdomen with a red river running out through her bloody fingers clasped against the wound. Virginia quickly tore open Teresa's flight suit and applied a pressure bandage against the hole.

"How bad is it, Gini?" asked Teresa.

"You'll live," replied Virginia not really knowing the truth.

"I don't think our ship can stand another attack, Capt.," said Honey.

"You don't have to! We are right above you," came a voice on the open radio channel.

"Who is this?" responded Virginia clutching a microphone at her station.

"It's Cyndy Bowie and I'm here with my squadron of Lightning P-38s. Sorry I'm late. We had some business to take care of."

"Cyndy, you are on an unsecure channel. The Germans can hear you."

"Can't help it, Gini. The only channel I got."

"This is Commander Bowie, to all squadron leaders. The 12th and 14th squadron, take the left flank. The 11th and 13th, cover the right. The 15th and 16th, follow me in. Let's see how many of these Krauts we can chop up on our first pass!"

The Germans were listening in on Commander Cyndy Bowie's orders and did not want anything to do with so many fighters, especially P-38s so they quickly broke off their attack and hot-footed homeward. When Cyndy Bowie's speedy silver fighter flew past Virginia's plane, she was alone.

"Ahhh Cyndy, where's the rest of your flight?" asked Virginia.

"Oh them, I made them up."

They all heard the conversation and started to laugh. "Now that's a New Yorker," said Virginia.

B-25 Mitchell (1)

Just then a lone Fw-190 buzzed passed their plane letting loose a barrage of shells. "Virginia, Julie has been hit again," said Teresa.

Virginia made her way through the tunnel to see Julie lying against the bulkhead with a whole in her chest where her heart used to be. She was starring off into space. Tears welled up in Virginia's eyes. "Florida has lost one of its best daughters," she said quietly.

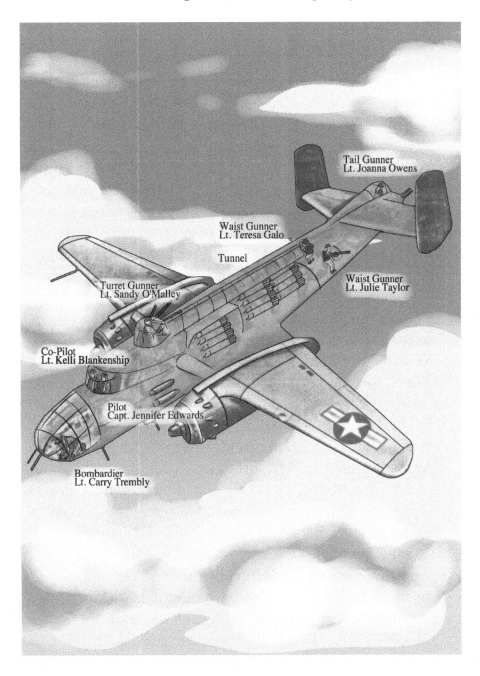

INTRO

World War II was the single most violent and destructive conflict in human history. Historians are still counting the dead some 73 years later. Due to the fall of the Soviet empire and due to newly released and declassified papers made available for easy access through the internet, the total today is upwards 70 million killed including civilian and service personnel. The war was the result of unsettle hard feelings and issues left over from the previous World War.

At the end of WWI, Central Europe was in ruin and the world blamed the Germans. Even though Germany was never hit by even one artillery shell, the German generals opted to cease hostilities. Their ability to sustain the conflict had been severely impeded by an extensive use of all its resources. In addition, The US entered the war with one million fresh, but green, troops and 1700 new and modern warplanes.

The Treaty of Versailles, the agreement that ended World War I, left much resentment in Germany. Germany was forced to surrender its foreign colonies in Africa. In addition, Germany ceded its border territories, Alsace and Lorraine, to France. Germany was forced to pay huge war reparations creating discord and much discontent amongst the war veterans and the populace.

Then there was The Great Depression of the 1930s creating further country-wide economic hardships and fear of massive unemployment. The value of the Deutch mark (Germany's currency) plummeted to 4.5 million to one American Dollar. Inflation in Germany ran rampant.

A loaf of bread cost half a million German marks. The Germans took wheel barrows full of money to the market. The country was in turmoil giving Adolf Hitler his chance to rise to power.

Hitler overturned the Versailles Treaty, solved the country's economic woes, and returned Germany to a great power in Central Europe. So naturally the German people gave him absolute power.

WW II could have easily been avoided if France and England would have stepped up and taken decisive action against Hitler when he violated the Treaty of Versailles. Hitler's troops marched into the Rhineland, occupied Austria and annexed Czechoslovakia while France and England lacked the resolution to stop Germany. Simple intervention would have put the brakes on Der Fuehrer. Ultimately, France and England were not at all prepared for Hitler's onslaught.

World War II lasted in Europe from September 1, 1939 to May of 1945 when Hitler shot himself in his bunker in Berlin. (Yes he shot himself. Believing he escaped to Argentina is pure fantasy.) The war ended with staggering statistics. Approximately 3% of the world population and up to 40% of some nation's populations were dead. In addition to being shelled or bombed, most of the civilian deaths were due to starvation or disease. An unbelievable 60% to 100% of large cities were devastated by bombing and artillery. In the German city of Hamburg, 40,000 inhabitants were by aerial bombing.

City of Hamburg

In four short decades, a species that had just learned how to fly gathered huge aerial armadas capable of pounding an entire city into rubble. In 80 years, that same species went from fighting with sabers and single shot muskets…to delivering a single bomb from a single plane that destroyed a single city with all of its inhabitants. There is no telling what this species will do next.

The war is over for most, but not all. There is a large collection of undetonated ordnance still hidden under the towns and cities in Russia, Poland, France, Belgium, even the US and especially Germany. Many times, during construction of roads and houses, a huge unexploded bomb dropped from an allied aircraft would be found in Germany. Large populations are quickly evacuated. Most bombs are successfully disarmed. Many result in explosions and those nearby, such as the bomb squad or a German who thought it smart to tinker with a 551 pound bomb, are killed.

B-17 Flying Fortress

During the war, the city of Oranienburg, about an hour north of Berlin, was the location of a factory that built the jet powered Messerschmitt 263, as well as the research facility for the German atomic bomb, and a railroad connection to move troops. It was also an important main target for the United States Army Air Force.

On one day, the US sent 2000 American B-17 bombers (heavies) to level Oranienburg. The planes stretched from horizon to horizon. They dropped 5,700 bombs in just 45 minutes. Normally, 20 % of the bombs dropped had a crude time delay detonator; however, on that day 50 % were time delayed. Many did not explode at all.

Today, experts believe that there are as many as 300…551 pound bombs still unexploded in Oranienburg with some clustered close to one another. Since 2008, an aggressive search has been done there using aerial photos taken by the Americans and British. A local man found one under his house while building an addition. After the bomb squad could not defuse the bomb, it had to be detonated, destroying the man's house.

In addition to searching for bombs, there are dozens of groups and organizations from Europe and the US who search documented mass grave sites and airplane crash sites for deceased military and civilian personnel. Much of the time they are successful of unearthing 50 or more persons at one site. A human body is easy to spot. While the earth movers gingerly remove layers of soil six inches at a time, the usually light brown soil suddenly turns dark. Aha, there they are. Then there is the less than glamorous, grisly task of identifying the corpses.

¥

At the onset of the war, the lack of manpower was quickly realized by most of the major Belligerents leading to the reluctant large scale use of the nation's daughters in the military. Women were a large resource of able bodies needed to fill supporting roles so to free up another man for combat. The women demonstrated a need to defend their homeland just as much as the men. Some nations, such as the US, denied their women the right of retribution based on antiquated ideas. Other countries embraced their ladies' fighting spirit.

CHAPTER 2

THE GERMANS

One would think, wouldn't one, that the Germans would be the first to send their women into air combat, what with all the "Ride of the Valkyrie" and all, the opera by Richard Wagner. The Valkyrie represented Nordic Goddesses who flew fallen German war heroes to Valhalla. This concept is far from the truth. Prior to WW II, Turkey was the only country to put a woman behind the controls of a warplane.

Sabiha Gokcen (2)

The honor of being the first female combat pilot belongs to Sabiha Gokcen of Turkey. Gokcen enlisted in the Turkish Air Force in 1936 at the age of 23. In 1938, she flew bombing, not fighter, missions against Kurdish rebels. Gokcen logged 30 combat hours bombing Kurdish positions in a very unpopular time in Turkish history. Today, the war on the Kurds is viewed as cruel and inhumane.

In 1939, when the Germans poured over its Eastern border into Poland, marking the start of WW II, there were few women in the military and none in combat in any nation.

Finland, and then Romania, (both aligned with Germany) started a small branch of their military to employ women as nurses, air raid wardens and hospital workers. The German philosophy towards their women was that they should stay home, take care of the house and raise children for the Reich. Only a small percentage worked in the factories.

In the 1940s, the Germans formed (get ready for this word) The Luftnachrichten-helferinnen. They were women in a branch of the Luftwaffe (German Air Force).

Luftnachrichten-helferinnen (3)

Like most countries, these women worked as secretaries, nurses and housekeepers. Later, as the war progressed, these women were assigned more important roles by the Luftwaffe such as radar station operators, signal corps and spotters for the anti-aircraft batteries. They freed up men to fight at the front. The German women were well respected by the German populace. They were promoted and glorified by the Propaganda Ministry as heroes unlike in other countries, USA. The ladies in the Luftwaffe wore smart looking uniforms tailored just for them.

One German aviatrix stood out from the rest. Though she never saw combat, at the end of the war she had to fly herself out of harm's way while dodging Russian anti-aircraft fire and while being chased by Russian Yak-9's (a very sophisticated Russian fighter plane, flew circles around the American P-51 Mustang).

Hanna Reitsch (4)

Hanna Reitsch was as fearless and was as talented as any ace. She initially claimed fame as Hitler's lady test pilot in the years before the war. Reitsch tested Germany's new warplanes such as the Stuka dive bomber and the Dornier Do-17 bomber. She was promoted and glorified by German propaganda.

Hanna Reitsch's forte was gliders. Gliders were small aircraft without any engines con-sisting of 10 soldiers. They were towed over the battle field by a larger plane then released to glide to earth. Reitsch presented a plan to Hitler to use 41 silent gliders to assault the seemingly impenetrable fortress Fort Eben-emael on the Belgium/German frontier.

Hitler approved the pretty 28 year old Fraulien Reitsch's plans and in the early hours of May 10th 1940, Germany invaded the declared neutral country of Belgium with paratroopers and ground forces supported by a squadron of 30 silent troop carrying gliders. Each glider carried a dozen soldiers. One glider landed on the grassy top of the Fortress Fort Eben-emael, needles to say the garrison was quickly overwhelmed. Reitsch did not actually take part in the invasion but was probably on the sidelines monitoring the progress.

Messerschmitt 163 Komet

Later during the war, Hanna Reitsch was one of the many test pilots of the Messerschmitt 163 Komet rocket engine plane. The Komet was years ahead of it time. It had no propeller being powered by a hydrogen peroxide motor to speeds in excess of 600 miles per hour. The inherent dangers of flying this experimental plane were real. Many test pilots were killed.

Veteran test pilot and Reitsch's friend, Heini Hittmar, was hospitalized after a crash but not before he pressed the Komet to speeds beyond 660 MPH. On Reitsch's fifth test flight, there was a landing gear malfunction and she crashed on take off. Hanna Reitsch survived the crash but with head injuries and sans a nose but after 5 months in the hospital, she was back in the cockpit.

As the Russian army closed in on Hitler's bunker in Berlin, in May 1945, Hanna Reitsch was ordered to fly the newly appointed head of the Luftwaffe, Robert Ritter von Greim, to Potsdamer Platz, Germany. Reitsch navigated an AR 96 through a hail of Russian anti-aircraft fire and eluded a few Yak-9s to escape Berlin.

Reitsch and von Greim were both captured by the Americans. Von Greim sucked on a cyanide pill. Reitsch was given the option of assisting the Americans or go to jail. She spent the next 18 months in an American prison only to go home and discover that her bat crap crazy father could not live in a defeated Germany and murdered Hanna's three sisters before killing himself. Reitsch survived the war and continued to fly all around the globe (but never in America). She passed in 1978 at the old age of 67.

CHAPTER 3

THE RUSSIANS

Unlike the rest of the world, Russia was a wealth of equal opportunities for all. Their women were permitted to do anything or be anything they wanted to be: scientists, stateswomen, engineers or pilot. Marina Raskova, at the age of 28, was a Major in the Soviet Air Force in June 1941 when 3 million German troops flowed over the German/Russian frontier. Maj. Raskova, who knew General Secretary Joseph Stalin (leader of the Soviet Union), petitioned The General Secretary about forming an all women air combat squadron.

Maj. Marina Raskova (6)

At the time, the Soviet army was in shambles and in full retreat. The grounded air force was being pounded by German Messerschmitt 109's (Me-109) who ruled the sky. Russia did not have a shortage of pilots but still Stalin had no qualms about throwing Russia's daughters into harm's way.

In October of 1941, an order was handed to Major Raskova to form a squadron consisting of only women, including the mechanics and engineers. She started the fighter 586th squadron which was a defensive unit who protected Russian bombers. They flew the sophisticated YAK-1 and the LaGG-3 fighter planes.

Lydia 'Lilly' Litvyak (her name even says fighter pilot) had to embellish (lie about) her prewar flight experience to enlist into the Air Force. The Jewish born 19 year old from Moscow, started flying for the 586th in late 1941. It was not long before her skills and talents; and the talents of some of the other female pilots, were quickly noticed.

Lilly Litvyak, along with Katya Budanova, Mariya Kuznetsova, Raisa Beliaeva and some female mechanics were transferred to a men's combat unit, the 437th Fighter Regiment, in the September of '42 to defend Stalingrad. Litvyak was promoted to Lieutenant. Three days after her transfer, Lt. Litvyak scored her first two kills, a Junker 88 bomber and a Messerschmitt 109 escort. She became the first female fighter pilot to shoot down an enemy aircraft.

The Me-109 was a sophisticated aircraft but in the early part of the war it had not come into its own and was comparable to the Yak-1. For a third world nation that could not make a decent toaster…the Russians built some really fine airplanes.

Messerschmitt Me-109 (7)

In September, Litvyak and her wing woman, Katya Budanova, attacked an incoming squadron of German Junker 88 bombers. Katya Budanova had her first assist, sharing a kill with Lt. Litvyak. In the first week of October 1942, Katya Budanova got her first solo kills, a Junker 88 and a Messerschmitt 109 on the same day.

Lt. Litvyak is third from left

Budanova was tall and described as 'a cheerful, lively character' whilst Litvyak was 'always thoughtful and quiet'.

¥

While the 586th was flying escorts, Maj. Raskova selected girls as young as 17 from Soviet air clubs for a bomber group. After six months of training they were rushed to Stalingrad and in June, 1942, they became the 588 bomber squadron.

The 588th flew harassment and precision bombing missions over German front lines at Stalingrad. They bombed encampments, supply depots and rear base areas. Their constant nighttime bombing made life very difficult for the Germans.

Po-2 (9)

The 588th was given very old and obsolete bi-planes called Polikarpov 2 (Po-2). The Po-2 was originally a crop duster before the Russian Air Force used it as a trainer. These planes were simple with a duo open cockpit. The pilot was in the front and the navigator/bombardier was in the back. The Po-2 was 27 feet long with a 37 foot wing span, made out of plywood with a canvas skin. Its top speed was 100 mph and had a cruising speed of 68. The dashboard did include a gas gauge, altimeter and airspeed indicator. In addition, the navigator had a bombsite to aim the bombs.

One would think that the Russian Air Force gave the women the worst planes that were available, but that could not be further from the truth. After the German invasion, the Russian Air Force had plenty of pilots but its planes were reduced to scrap metal. The women were lucky to receive any planes at all. In the end, the Po-2 was the best plane for what the women had to do.

The Russian women would fly only at night. They approached their target at tree top level before climbing to 1500 feet to make their bomb run. At 1500, the pilot cut the clanky noisy engine and silently glided over the target making no sound. The pilot kept the aircraft steady while the bombardier took aim. After releasing their bombs, the pilot started the engine and dropped back to the tree tops to return home. A pair of women with one plane did that 10 times a night. The Germans dubbed the women 'Nachthexen', (Night Witches) because of the whooshing sound the wind made in the supports on their planes. After they heard the whispering of the wind through the wires of the Po-2…they heard harp music.

Because the women flew so low, the German fighters could not see them. Because the women flew so slow, the German fighters could not shoot them. The top speed of the Po-2 was 25 MPH slower than the German fighter's stall speed. The sophisticated Messerschmitt 109 (Me-109) had only a few seconds to get a bead on the Russian girls. When a Me-109 tried to intercept the Po-2, the Russian girl would throttle back and bank hard to starboard. The German would be forced to make a wide turn around the Po-2. When the German came back around, he was unable find the Po-2. If he did, the Russian girl repeated the maneuver until the German ran low on fuel or gave up and headed for home. Any German pilot who downed a Po-2 was promised an Iron Cross.

Like others in other air forces, the Russian women had casualties. A total of 30 planes were shot down over their four year history. Since the crew had no parachutes, and flew too low to use them anyhow, 43 Russian women died. There were 23 "Hero of the Soviet Union" medals awarded to the 588th, the highest distinction in the Soviet Union.

It must have been terrifying for an 18 year old girl flying over the German lines. It was terribly cold. The German search lights had to be blinding and then the anti-aircraft would cut loose on the small plane. It was hellish for the pilot who had to keep the plane steady, while being shot at, so the bombardier could get a fix before dropping two 200 pound bombs.

Off duty "Night Witches (10)

Many heroes came out of the 588th. Two women 20 year old Nadezhda Popova and Yekaterina Ryabova, flew 18 sorties in one night. When the women of the 588th returned to their airfield, they went into their huts to warm up and indulge in a hot chocolate-toffee elixir before they went back off in their Po-2. After a short respite, the Russian women returned to their planes which were refueled and rearmed, the oil was checked and the windshield cleared. They then returned to the night sky to bomb the crap out of the Germans.

The Russian women were doing well until January 1943 when the unthinkable happened. Their commander, then Colonel Marina Raskova, died in a training accident while flying the new dive bomber, the Petlyakov or Pe-2. Raskova was 30 years old at the time of her death. She had organized the third women's squadron, the 587 Bomber Group and was given the new air plane (Pe-2) even before the men's group had it.

Col. Marina Raskova's death was shocking news to the women. How were they to go on without their beloved leader? They pulled themselves together and soldiered on just as Raskova would have wanted. They flew their sorties. The 588th was offered the new Pe-2s but the women chose to keep their Po-2s...maybe because their leader met her demise in the new aircraft.

Whilst the 588th was bombing the Germans at night, Lt. Lilly Litvyak and Lt. Katya Budanova were downing German incoming bombers. By January 1943, Litvyak was credited with 10 kills and 4 assists. She and Budanova were chosen for the elite Free Hunters. Those were fighter pilots who were permitted to roam the skies at the front looking for incoming enemy planes.

Lt. Litvyak was better known to the Germans than to her own people. When a German bomber pilot saw the white lily (It was a lily) painted on the side of her Yak 1, they immediately dropped their bombs where ever they were and turned toward home. The Me-109 pilots opted not to engage Lt. Litvyak once they noticed the ever familiar 73 on the tail of her plane.

Ju-88 Lt. Litvyak victim (11)

Lt. Litvyak was a beautiful woman with short hair that she bleached blond. Even though she served in a 'man's role' she never acted like it. She did her make up using her navigation pencil as eye liner. She picked wild flowers and kept them in her cockpit on missions only to be tossed while her plane was serviced between sorties. The Russian Propaganda Ministry liked Litvyak and Budanova because little touch up was needed on their pictures when the they were glorified in newspapers and magazines on the home front.

Yak-1 (12)

In February of '43, they each took on new wing men. Budanova flew with Nikolai Baranov and Litvyak flew with Kapitain Alexei Solomatin. Lt. Litvyak became very fond of her wing man and they were secretly engaged. In May of '43, while coming back from a mission, she witnessed her fiancée, Kapitain Solomatin, get shot down by a Me-109. She was heart broken. From then on, Litvyak only flew combat missions.

In July of '43, Budanova was in a heated dogfight with a squadron of Me-109's. She was credited with 2 kills before her plane was peppered by a third. She managed to land the Legg-3 in a field but when the farmers got to her she had died from her wounds at the age of 26. Katya Budanvova totaled 6 kills and 4 assists in her career.

Lilly Litvyak's final mission was in August 1943. She was attacking a squadron of Junker 88 bombers when she was jumped by two Me-109's. Litvyak just did not see them before they closed in on her plane. Instead of diving, she turned to encounter the 109's. A witness, Ivan Borisenko, a Soviet pilot engaged in the ensuing dogfight said, "She disappeared in the clouds with eight Me-109's on her tail. Lt. Litvyak appeared through a gap in the clouds and her Yak-1 was smoking." Lt. Litvyak never returned from the mission. Lt. Lilly Litvyak is credited with a life time total of 13 kills and 4 assists. She was the first woman ace and holds the record for the most kills by a female pilot. Lt. Lilly Litvyak died 2 weeks before her 22nd birthday.

Lt. Lilly Litvyak

CHAPTER 4

THE WOMEN OF FINLAND

Between 1939 and 1945, the Soviet Union's attempt to 'annex' Finland met with repeated and severe failures mostly because of Finland's resistance and mostly because Soviets failed to realize that the Finish women were extremely tenacious much like their own Russian women. In November, 1939, two months after Germany poured into Poland, Russia invaded Finland without provocation. The results were disastrous for the Soviets.

The Russians were ill prepared to wage a war in Finland's bitter arctic cold winter and the Fins put up a much more formidable defense than the Russians assumed they could. The Russians invaded with one million troops out of which 200,000 were killed and many of the survivors suffered from frost bite. The Fins lost only 25,000 troops but a cession of hostilities came in March of 1940.

Not long after Hitler invaded Russia in June of 1941 (Operation Barbarossa), the Russians once again attacked Finland. Finland aligned itself, but did not ally itself with Germany. What else could a mostly agricultural country with a population of less than 3 million do against a larger and more powerful foe? There is no proof but one can bet that the Germans poured men and hardware into Finland to fight the Russians. Once again the Russians were repulsed with heavy casualties.

Toward the end of the war, in 1944, the Russians attacked yet again with similar results.

In the peace treaties that followed the end of the war, Finland was royally screwed, most likely due to its relationship with Germany. It was forced to give up its only industry to the Russians and make war reparations even though Russia was clearly the aggressor. Finland became democratic and secretly aligned itself with the US.

Lotta-Svärd Air Raid Spotters (13)

Another reason Russia fared so poorly in their bid to conquer Finland was due to Finland's Lotta-Svärd. Lotta-Svärd was an all women's paramilitary organization that was formed after Finland's independence in 1918. The women of the Lotta-Svärd worked in hospitals, as air raid wardens and performed other auxiliary tasks in conjunction with the armed forces. In the massive 1944 Russian invasion, the Lotta-Svärd operated anti-aircraft batteries at Helsinki (Finland's capital city) and at the front. The women were issued rifles and side arms in the event the Russians broke through the lines.

Due to the efforts of the Lotta-Svärd, 100,000 men were freed up for active military service. (I bet they enjoyed the crap out of that) By the end of the war, the Lotta-Svärd was a quarter of a million strong in a country of 3 million inhabitants. Lotta-Svärd suffered 241 deaths half in combat and half due to illnesses. Their fallen were buried with full military honors in a hero's cemetery.

¥

A note from the author:

I have included emblems and cap badges for a few organizations in this book. I would like to include the insignia for the quarter of a million Finnish women who fought for their country but I can not by law. The Lotta-Svärd's symbol consists of four roses that surround a swastika and NOT because Finland aligned itself with the Nazis.

The Lotta-Svärd's emblem was approved in 1921 while Hitler was a nobody. To the people of Finland, the swastika was a symbol of luck, success, wellness and prosperity. It was Hitler who made the swastika a symbol of fear, hatred and terror that makes people so uncomfortable today.

In the past, the Buddhist, Hindu and other Eastern religions used the swastika in their art to wish one another well. The symbol spread into the modern Scandinavian countries of Sweden, Norway and FINLAND then on into Northern England. The

American Indians also had a swastika in their art work. It was a true swastika called a rolling log or sometimes called whirling log. The symbol was used in healing rituals. The use of the rolling log symbol is limited today. How do two distinctly different cultures separated by a vast ocean and 10,000 miles have identical symbols?

Noted astronomer Carl Sagan answered that question in his book titled 'Comet'. Around 200 BC a comet came exceptionally close to Earth. Due to the comet's rotation, and Earth's gravitational pull, the tail divided into fourths. As the comet spun the tails bent forming a swastika. Because of the rotation of the Earth and its relationship to the comet in the night sky, the Native Americans and the Buddhists saw the same comet on the same night. I reckon since the comet did not impact the Earth, people thought it was a good sign or lucky.

So the Lotta-Svärd, being Scandinavian and all, used the same symbol of luck, wellness, prosperity, good fortune, success I could go on but I will come to the point. The Lotta-Svärd used the swastika with a silver rose in the four corners in their insignia.

I would like to display the Lotta-Svärd insignia but I can not because, I am not making this up, the insignia was banned by the Federal Constitution Court of Germany. The use of the Lotta-Svärd's symbol in Germany, Austria, Hungary, Poland, Brazil, Israel and a host of other nations is <u>illegal</u>. Since I would like to return to Germany without being thrown into a Deutsch hoosegow and made into some big German boy's fraulein, I will cave to the German law and omit the fine fighting Finnish women's insignia.

In downtown Fort Myers, Florida, there is a night club at the end of Patio Deleon. It is upscale and carpeted now but in the early '80s it had a tile floor. I used to frequent the establishment often and could not help but notice that the tile floor was bordered by smaller tiles with swastikas on them. The building was constructed in the 20s.

The Native Americans also caved to the German courts. In the 1940's, an Indian counsel opted to limit the use of the rolling log. In August, 2017, a group of tourists were visiting a flea market in Salt Lake City and found a woven blanket displaying a large rolling log in the center. Imagine…a blanket with healing powers…can I get one on Amazon?

Well anyhow, these tourists did not take a few seconds to wonder why the Native Americans would put a White supremacist symbol on their blankets. Instead, the ignorant gaggle yelled, screamed and hollered at the store owner leading to further protest outside the flea market. Maybe Utah needs a wall to keep short sighted ignorant tourist at bay.

Those who protest rolling logs on blankets and those who protest the Lotta Svärd's symbol should step back and heed the words of Star Trek's Counselor Deanna Troi, (S7:E6) 'Data, sometimes a cake is just a cake.'

CHAPTER 4

THE WOMEN ROMANIA

In Romania, Princess Marina Stirbey had read about the Lotta-Svärd and formed the Escadrila Alba aka the White Squadron. Like Finland, Russia invaded Romania at the beginning of WW II. Like Finland, Romania turned to Germany for assistance after Operation Barbarossa. The Soviet invasion was repelled; however, the Germans received Romania's agricultural benefits (fourth in Europe), oil production (seventh in the world) and military assistance a 1.2 million man army.

In 1939, aviatrix Princess Marina Stirbey organized the White Squadron. The White Squadron was an air borne ambulance unit that delivered whole blood and other medical supplies to the Romanian army at Stalingrad then ferried severely wounded soldiers back to mobile medical units near the front. This was 11 years before Alan Alda and M*A*S*H.

White Squadron RWD-13 (14)

The White Squadron began with only four female pilots, but by the end of the war their numbers swelled to 21. Not much is written about the White Squadron because heroes from the war were suppressed by the communist government that took over after the war. The existence of the White Squadron has only recently become more widely known. In 2013, the final member of the squadron, Commander Mariana Dragescu, passed away at the age of 100.

Lt. Mariana Dragescu (15)

The White Squadron flew small airplanes captured from Poland called RWD-13's. Originally, the planes were painted white, had German insignias but included a big red cross on the wings and fuselage signifying it was on a medical mission. However, the Russian pilots used the red cross as a target firing on the White Squadron's planes. Ergo, the white planes were painted the usual camouflage color.

The White Squadron was engaged in Stalingrad, Odessa and the Crimean offensives. They flew in at tree top level to avoid detection however they could not avoid being shot at by Russian ground units. While on the ground, the Romanian girls gave their mess kits to any starving Russian children they encountered. They are credited with air lifting and saving 1500 Romanian soldiers.

CHAPTER 5

THE BRITISH ATA GIRLS AND AUXILIARY TERITORIAL SERVICE

The British did not put their women in combat, at least not directly, however, many of their women ferried warplanes from the factories to the airbases. The Air Transport Auxiliary (ATA) was composed of 1300 flyers 168 of who were women. The ATA had its own unit that flew for the RAF (Royal Air Force). Their home base was in Hampshire, though they had bases in five different locales in England, usually near a factory, an aircraft repair depot or maintenance units where the guns were fitted on the war birds. The ATA freed-up much needed pilots to defend the island country from incoming German bombers.

The women's group was formed and led by Pauline Gower. Ms. Gower took charge of selecting and training the ladies for the ATA, or 'AT-A-Girls' as they were later dubbed. There was no sex discrimination in the ATA. The women were paid the same as their male counterparts, unlike other countries, USA.

The ATA girls came from 25 nations. Florida-born Jacqueline Cochran led 25 American girls who joined the ATA. Cochran and a few of the ladies returned to the US to start the WASP program. Among the American women was Helen Richey who enlisted in the ATA on her own.

Diana Walker At-A-Girl (16)

In 1940, 92% of the Americans felt that WW II was a European war and America should stay out of it. So if a woman was to fly war planes, she would have to go to England and enlist in the RAF. After the Japanese sneak attack on Pearl Harbor on Dec. 7th 1941, 92% of the Americans wanted pay back on the Axis. Helen Ritchey did not wait until Hitler declared war on her home town of Mc Keesport, Pennsylvania and went off to England.

American Girl Ritchey (17)

Helen Ritchey received her pilot's license in 1929 at the age of 20. In the 1930s, Ritchey partnered up with her friend Amelia Earhart and competed in air races and set altitude and endurance records. She went to work for Central Airlines as the first Female airline pilot but was forced out of the cockpit when the company went to an all male union in 1936. Ms. Richey joined the ATA in 1940 and stayed for the duration of the war.

The ATA ferried 38 different types of aircraft from Spitfires to heavy bombers. When the ATA girls delivered a large bomber, the base commander would look to find the real pilot. The RAF did not want any of the ATA pilots to fly in adverse conditions, but later during the war, the ATA girls were permitted to fly over the channel in search of Axis ships and submarines. A total 15 ATA girls died in accidents during the war.

It would be amiss not to mention the British Auxiliary Territorial Service. From the 9th of September 1938, every woman who joined the British army joined the Auxiliary Territorial Service or ATS.

ATS cap badge

In the beginning, the girls of the ATS were given the same typical women's work i.e. clerks, cooks, secretaries, but their responsibilities were expanded later to include RADAR operators, communication experts, search lights and even anti-aircraft crews. There were 300 ATS members stationed in France when the country crumbled in the path of the advancing German Army. The British women, as young as 17, kept the lines of communications open and were the last to leave the European continent during the evacuation of Dunkirk.

By September of 1941, the ATS were 65,000 strong. In an effort to free up able bodied service men for combat, the ATS were trained to operate RADAR, search lights and anti-aircraft batteries. These women saw their share of action resulting in 717 casualties during WW II.

Once again the allies trained their daughters to get out and do semi-dangerous jobs while defending their country. All the allies except one, guess who…the USA, where all are created equal.

CHAPTER 6

THE AMERICANS

All the European nations involved in WWII were proud of their brave women who sacrificed themselves for their country. They glorified their women in propaganda and called them heroes...then there were the Americans. Tsk..Tsk...Tsk. The public opinion in the 1940's was so dead fast set against American women having anything to do with anything related to the military. Sure, women were 'allowed' to be riveters in factories turning out warplanes and tanks, however, the 'I Love Lucy' sentiment frowned on allowing women to actually fly those planes, let alone allowing them to fly in combat. Unheard of!

At the onset of WW II American Army and Navy nurses were stationed in Manila, Philippines. The United States Army Nurse Corps (USANC) was the nursing service for the US Army. If a woman was a nurse in the Army, she was in the USANC. The US Navy had a similar unit called The United States Navy Nurse Corp. Both units were composed of only registered nurses (RNs).

On December 8th 1941, Manila was bombed by the Japanese without a declaration of war. At the end of December, 88 nurses were ordered to evacuate Manila to the island fortresses of Corregidor and Bataan. A total of a dozen Army and Navy nurses stayed behind to continue caring for patients at Sternberg General Hospital. One nurse escaped before Manila fell…the other 11 were captured by the Japs.

On April 9th 1942, Bataan was surrendered to Japan. The American nurses were relocated to Corregidor which capitulated on April 29th. A small group of Army nurses escaped by sea plane but were stranded on Mindanao, the Philippines' second largest island, when the plane developed engine trouble. They became prisoners of the Japanese and shipped back to Manila. A few Army and one Navy nurse were evacuated by submarine.

During their years of interment, the American nurses continued caring for the sick and wounded as best as they could. They had few medicines to work with and even less equipment. After three and a half years, all the American nurses were liberated and sent home.

¥

In the early days of 1941, before Pearl Harbor, a congresswoman named Edith Rogers recalled how the women who served in WW I did not share in the benefits given to veterans such as disability benefits or pensions. In addition, while serving with the Army, the women had to obtain their own food, housing and received no medical benefits. If they were captured, the American women were really up a creek because since they were civilians, they were not protected by the Geneva Convention. Ms. Rogers presented a bill which would give those women serving with the military all the rights and benefits as the men.

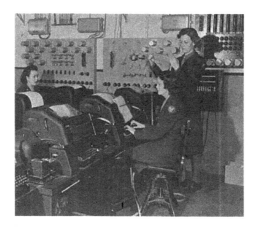

WAC at work

Congress passed Ms. Roger's bill in May of '41, 6 months before Pearl, over 25,000 women were recruited for the newly formed Women's Army Auxiliary Corps (WAAC). The bill provided for the women's food, quarters, clothing, medical care and pay but not as much as the men made, of course. The first director was Oveto Hobby, the wife of a former Texas Governor. Among the tasks of the WAAC recruits were switchboard operators, clerical specialists, nurses, mechanics, teachers, stenographers and secretaries.

After Pearl Harbor, and after the Germans declared war on the US, America was plunged into a two-front war. The supply of suitable manpower was not fully meeting the need. The women of the WAAC did jobs that would free up a man for combat. Later, the "A" was dropped and the organization was called the WAC.

To fill the need for additional women to serve in the WAC, a nation-wide recruiting campaign was launched. Posters were dawn up and radio ads were played across the country. It was cut short though due to negative public opinion. The US sentiment was that the American girl was only good for staying home to cook, clean, do laundry and raise children. Many Americans feared that with women doing the soft safe jobs, their loved ones would have to serve in combat. Then the Americans challenged the service woman's moral sexually being in uniform. The US populace on the home front went so far as to call the WACs lesbians, whores and prostitutes. Those were American women serving their country in the military.

The WAC officially became a part of the Army on July 4th 1943. The women serving were given the option of staying in the Army or going home; 75% stayed.

¥

In 1939, as the German Blitz Krieg pounded Poland, Florida born Jacqueline Cochran appealed to Eleanor Roosevelt requesting the US Military employ female pilots. In May of 1940, Nancy Love had the same idea and wrote to the existing Ferrying Division of the US

Army Air Force to employ women. Both plans were rejected. Cochran went to England with 26 American women to fly for the ATA.

After Pearl Harbor, there was a lack of pilots in the US so Cochran returned to the US with three female pilots. In 1942, General Henry "Hap" Arnold, Commander General of the American Army Air Force, approved a plan to train women to fly the Army way. They did not receive any combat training; however they were taught how to get out of adverse situations. Command of the Women's Flying Training Detachment (WFTD) was given to Jacqueline Cochran.

Approximately 25,000 women, all of whom already had pilot's licenses, applied with the WFTD. Of those 25,000…1900 women were chosen to train in Huston, Texas where 1074 made the grade. In August of 1943, the WFTD and Nancy Love's women working for the Ferrying Division merged to form the Woman's Air Force Service Pilots, or the WASP.

WASP's L to R Green, Kirchner, Walden & Osborn in Ohio

The WASP logged over 60 million miles flying an array of warplanes such as the P-38 Lightning, the P-47 Thunder Bolt and later, the P-51 Mustang. They also flew bombers like the B-17 Flying Fortress, B-25 Mitchell and the B-26 Marauder. The WASP flew the aircraft from the factories to the port of embarkation. The women also served as flight instructors, tow-target pilots and test pilots from 120 air bases across the US but not overseas.

WASP Deanie Parish

The WASP was a paramilitary group and was never a part of the Army. They paid for their own uniforms, lodging, food and personal travel to and from home. If they died while on duty, which 38 of them did, their families were responsible for all funeral expenses. Much of the time, the deceased WASP's family was too poor to ship their daughter home. The women in her unit would pass a hat until there was enough money to pay for a trip home. In addition, the family was not given a flag to drape over the coffin unlike the Finish women who were laid to rest with honors or the Russian women who received a hero's funeral!

An Act was presented before congress to militarize the WASP; however, just as the bill finally came up for discussion, the need for the women pilots had diminished. The WASPs were disbanded on December 20, 1944 with no thanks, no fanfare nor a bus ticket home. They did receive a hearty thanks from Gen. Henry 'Hap' Arnold. He was a class act.

Ergo, history teaches us that America did not have any women flying combat missions. This was due to the strong public opinion disapproving American women in combat in any way. The American women were just as angry about Pearl Harbor as the American men. They also wanted to destroy Japan and Germany. Over 25,000 American women volunteered to fly in combat. If Gen. Hap Arnold wanted to utilize those fierce fighting females.....

He had to do it in secret!!

CHAPTER 7

SEARCHING THE INTERNET

I am, of course, Bill Muntean and of no consequence except the only person, outside of those in this book, who knows what truly happened in the 1940s. I discovered this top secret tale after an extensive search of recently declassified 75 year old documents found on the internet.

While poring over the pages I concentrated my attention on those from the United States Army Air Force. (USAAF) I have been just a WW II aircraft nut since I was a kid. I admit, my living room looks like a museum with some 50 WW II model airplanes on display.

So anyhow, one evening I was watching a few videos on 'YouTube' about the take offs, landings and missions of some vintage WW II fighters and bombers. One video in particular pertained to the now disbanded 10th bomber group that was a supposedly an all male squadron in England. I asked myself, *'If it was all male why were there women at the controls of the war birds?'* Initially, I figured they were WASPs in Europe; however, I Googled the 10th and found nothing. Then I Googled the name of the airbase the 10th from which they flew from (this is called the backdoor) and there were more pixs of girls at the planes' 30 caliber machine guns.

So I ventured down this electronic rabbit hole of paper work pertaining to the USAAF and the 10th. Most of it was boring stuff that is common knowledge today but persistence paid off and I found something very interesting. I fell upon some paperwork signed by General Henry 'Hap' Arnold himself. Unlike most of the paperwork, these pages were marked 'Top Secret' and had some spaces blacked out, and most of it was in code.

Because of the coding, I moved on to more legible but far less interesting items. After a small while, I had to return to the coded pages, 49 sheets of what looked like a mumbled jumbled-up collection of capital and lower case letters except for all the two and three lettered words. What the hell, I printed the pages.

Once my HP LaserJet stopped humming, I stapled the collection of meaningless shits (I mean sheets) together and tossed the packet on a pile of other worthless junk. I had spent too much time on those pages already. It was time to move on so I shut off the computer and went to my favorite pub to meet up with some folks, shoot some pool and slam a few beers. After all it was a very special occasion…Wednesday!!!

The following evening I returned to the coded pages. I don't watch much television since becoming a writer. Cable has created a new low in low brow crap on T.V. The Kardashians. What's up with them? The first time I heard that the Kardashians had a new show, I thought it was a spin off of 'Star Trek: Deep Space 9.' After watching the show for five minutes I said aloud, "Those ain't no Cardassians and where is Nana Visitor?" No one could rock a Bajoran uniform like Nana Visitor. They should give her a reality show.

Sorry, I digress. I don't watch much T.V. since becoming a writer. I stared at the coded messages I printed the nite before. I rocked back and forth in my office chair studying the words in the document. I'm no genius; however I broke the simple code. If a word has the correct first letter and the correct last letter, the other letters in the word can be jumble in any fashion and the human mind will visualize the correct word. That is what the USAAF used to code the papers. As I translated the coded pages into legible English, a most bizarre and most impossible story unfolded.

The papers were a proposal written by a Major GD. The proposal spoke about the short sightedness of the gaggle that made up the American populace. American women flying combat aircraft was absolutely unthinkable. They could hardly be expected to keep office floors mopped so how could they fly sophisticated aircraft? And what of the American men? How would they react to sharing an airbase with a squadron of all women? However, 25,000 women wanted to join the WASP.

Major GD, whose name was repeated often, went on to state that the American girls could be trained to fly bombers and fighters and be just as formidable as well trained men. He may have developed this plan during the dark days of the USAAF when 40% of the B-17's sent to bomb Germany did not return. In addition, the 60% that did return were riddled by machine gun fire and flak and suffered heavy casualties. The planes fell victim to a sophisticated German fighter dubbed the Me-109s and anti-aircraft batteries that used German women as spotters. Spotters are just as the name suggests. The Germans used women in forward positions to identify incoming enemy bombers. Then they would radio the planes' positions, airspeed and altitude to the big guns.

In addition, the German women were also a part of the anti-aircraft crews. They could aim the ack-ack guns but were not allowed to pull the trigger…that would not be lady like.

Maj. GD recognized that there was a large unused pool of talent available to the USAAF. He realized that there was nothing an all male bomber crew could do that a well trained all female crew could not do. In addition, the women were smaller in stature than the men thus weighed less so they could carry more bombs or more fuel than the men. Major GD presented his concept of organizing an all women combat squadron to General "Hap" Arnold. Arnold approved the plan not because the air force was in need of talent, that too, but because he felt the women should be permitted to join the fray. However the country was involved in a major conflict. To announce that the USAAF was sending American women in harms way could have (the hell it would have) create a fire storm of controversy over the abilities of our High Command. There was already a war on two fronts…the US did not need another war on the home front. An all women squadron had to be formed in secret to avoid public ridicule.

The proposal was followed by a semblance of plans, contingence plans and reports of the progress of the training of the women. The final pages announced the formation of the 10th Bomber Squadron, as well as the 366th Fighter Squadron. The list of those approved to be American Bomber Girls was included in the USAAF pages. After further exhausting and frustrating research…of all the women who participated in this experiment, only one woman was still alive today.

Virginia White, now Virginia Morgenstern, was living in Marin County outside of San Francisco.

I felt an interview was necessary to find out all the details of her life as an American Bomber Girl. I could call Ms. Morgenstern on the phone so she could hang up on me. Nope the only way to confront the lady was in person…I had to go the California.

CHAPTER 8

MEETING A LEGEND

While being bounced around like a sack of potatoes on the plane ride over the Gulf of Mexico, there was time to look over the dossier I prepared on Virginia Morgenstern. Folks say I have a vivid imagination; however I was having a problem finding a way to make Ms. Morgenstern speak with me. Since her retirement, Ms. Morgenstern has become a bit of a recluse so people can't just walk up to her door and say 'Hey, tell me about the days you were in a top secret bomber squadron!!'

Ms. Morgenstern was a mere 14 years old when she left her home in Canton, Ohio to serve her country. There has to be a good story about that. After the American Girl mustered out of the Army Air Force in 1946, she returned to Ohio just long enough to change from her Captain uniform into some civvies. From there she moved about as far away from Canton as one could go…San Francisco, California.

Fortunately, Ms. Morgenstern is easy to track on Google. Since her departure from the army, she was very active in military related activities such as the USO, the V.A., the Red Cross, groups pushing for Military benefits for the WASPs and groups advocating women's advancement in the military. There was still nothing said about her tour with the 10th Bomber Group.

Things did not go real well for Ms. Morgenstern after arriving at San Francisco. She found affordable housing but began burning through her military back pay looking for a job. Even though she was a veteran, jobs for women were still few. The situation was becoming bleak until she met a lady who was a former Navy Wav during the war. They met at a USO function and immediately hit it off.

The lady owned and operated a successful travel agency right in downtown San Francisco. (There was a time when people relied on a business called a travel agency to book a trip on an airplane or cruise ship) Her name was Becky Hunter. Ms. Hunter was looking for an able woman to train as an assistant and then as a saleswoman. She gave Ms. Morgenstern a free place to live, in the finished basement of her house, and a job. They agreed to a low stipend until such time Ms. Morgenstern had learned the business and became a saleswoman.

Mastering the job did not take Ms. Morgenstern long. After four weeks she was promoted to saleswoman. She stayed with Hunter for three years before starting her own successful travel agency. Ms. Morgenstern went on to marry and have three children but always had time for her causes.

Still no reason for my visit and our flight was less than an hour from landing. Franticly searching the internet I finally found something. The American Bomber Girls, who navigated an armada of bombers to their target and then home again, couldn't drive. Sure she climbed behind the wheel of the car but she had an ambulance constantly following her and an abundance of traffic violations threatening her with loss of the driver's license. That was my "in".

¥

There are probably laws in California against impersonating a government official. I figured going back to Florida and never coming back to California would be the best course of action iffen I was caught. So I found a pay phone at the airport and phoned Virginia Morgenstern directly.

"Hello," came a girl's voice on the phone.

"Hello, this is Bill Muntean from the California Department of Motor Vehicles. May I speak with Virginia Morgenstern?" I felt silly; I have never done anything like that before.

"Just a minute," said the girl.

After a brief moment Ms. Morgenstern came to the phone. "Hello," answered the WW II hero.

"Hello Ms. Morgenstern, I'm Bill Muntean from the DMV and I discovered some discrepancies in your last visit. We need to correct these problems right away or you won't have a driver's license."

After a short argument on the phone, Ms. Morgenstern said she would come to the office in the morning to fill in the proper forms. "No, no, no," I said, "You shouldn't drive, I'll stop by this afternoon and we can do this paper work in your home. I have to be in your neighborhood later anyway."

"Well alright," she said.

"I'll see you at 3," I promised.

So I pull my rented Chevy Cruz up the driveway flanked on each side by a beautifully manicured lawn filled with flowering annuals, a gorgeous fountain surrounded by rock ornaments and huge loaded fruit trees. After parking the Cruz in front a sprawling ranch house, I went ahead and rang the doorbell. I was greeted by a drop dead gorgeous lady with a huge smile; brown eyes the size of golf balls. She was about my age. Her long thick brown hair, which fell past her shoulders, was sans a smidgen of gray. She wore a white sundress that waved around her knees with a plunging neck line that displayed the California girl's dark tan.

"Hello, I'm Bill Muntean from the DMV," I lied profusely. I was lucky to speak at all staring at the women's beautiful large…eyes, like a high school boy.

"Enchanté, Mr. Muntean, I am Jennifer, Virginia Morgenstern is my mother, we are expecting you. Please come in. My mother is in the atrium with her orchids. Follow me."

"You betcha, Jennifer," I replied.

As we passed through the living room I slowed to admire the vast collection of WW II war birds on display, many were the same ones I have. On another shelf were old pictures of women in American leather bomber jackets. There was a whole wall dedicated to the women each dressed in some semblance of air force uniform. Some individual pictures and others in group shots. Then there were pictures of the children…Ms. Morgenstern's children I correctly surmised.

Well I suppose I lingered to long because I was snapped out of my fugue state by Ms. Morgenstern standing before me with her arms folded across her chest. There she was…the great American war hero…now on in the years, but I was certain that this was not a frail old woman. She was 5'5" tall. Her once blond hair was still short but gray now. The American Bomber Girl was thin wearing a long denim skirt past her knees, a white shirt that buttoned in the front, and an Eisenhower cut blue denim jacket. Around her neck was a long thin white scarf similar to the ones the pilots in the war used to wear.

"Did you find something interesting, Mr. Muntean?" said Ms. Morgenstern.

"Well yes Ms. Morgenstern. I am interested in WW II airplanes. My living room is full of planes, too. Where did you get yours?"

"My son George built most of them since he was little. He is very good at it. The others I have purchased over the years when I see them."

"I noted a variety of B-25 Mitchell bombers. Is there a reason you are partial to that plane?"

Ms. Morgenstern stopped to think for a moment. "NO!! Mr. Muntean!" she said sternly, "No reason at all."

"These pictures are obviously your children. Is this George?" I asked.

"Yes that is my son George Daniel. That is Jennifer and the other girl is my youngest Taylor."

"Good looking bunch. I have one daughter and three grand children back…" I almost slipped. Better be more careful, this lady is no dummy. "Who are these other women in uniform?"

"I was a WASP during the war. These were the girls in my unit. Look here I am in this shot here," she said pointing herself out of a small group.

"Now I see where Jennifer gets her good looks."

"Actually, Jennifer favors her father. I was just in the atrium; I have a few things needing my attention. We can talk out there."

I accompanied the former flyer into a large greenhouse filled with fine orchids. Many were in bloom with a multitude of colorful flowers while others weren't. There were red, blue, green, and white flowers in two rows in the atrium.

"Ms. Morgenstern, you have a very nice collection. Do you know everything about them?"

"Please call me Gini. I know more about some than others."

"This purple one is nice. What's it called?" I asked.

"That is a Phalaenopsis. Its common name is Moth Orchid. It comes from the south Pacific region such as China, South India, and the Philippines. These red ones are of my favorites. They are called Epicedium. These are found from North Carolina to Argentina."

"This white one is unusual looking. What's it called?"

"That is a Miltonia from the rain forests of Brazil."

"I had no idea that orchids are so wide spread. We have an orchid that will only grow in our region called a Ghost…." Oh man, I am so bad at deceiving people, I slipped up again. This lady is an expert on exotic plants. Perhaps she did not catch my blunder.

"JENNIFER CALL THE POLICE!" announced Ms. Morgenstern. The expert caught my error. "The Ghost orchid only grows in the Fakahatchee Strand in south west Florida."

"Mom what's wrong?" asked Jennifer.

"I said call the police, this man is an imposter."

"Ms. Morgenstern, it is imperative that we speak. I am aware that you do not like visitors but…."

"I don't care what your reasons are, Mr. Muntean, if that is your real name. No matter, I'll let the local Sheriff sort things out." Ms. Morgenstern turned her back on me. "Jennifer, did you call the cops?"

"Is Jennifer named after Jennifer Edwards the Captain of 'The Angry Albatross', Ms. Morgenstern? Or should I say…Captain Virginia White? Your daughter Taylor is named after Lieutenant Julie Taylor. She died in your arms, didn't she? You weren't even supposed to be on that flight…were you? Your name was at the top of the duty rooster and you replaced the navigator Lieutenant Jetta Woodrell when she was too sick to fly."

The old woman froze and slumped over the top of a chair. She had lost all her composure, but only for a moment. The old woman stood up, adjusted her jacket and turned towards me.

"Mom…what is he talking about?" asked Jennifer in a quiet voice and her large eyes wide open.

"70 years later Ms. Morgenstern…and you could not even…tell…your own children. Isn't it about time?" I asked.

"Jennifer, phone the police and tell them everything is fine," instructed Ms. Morgenstern.

"Are you sure, Mom?"

"Quite sure, daughter."

Jennifer went to do as she was instructed.

"So Mr. Muntean, you seem to be well informed about me and my friends. You wanna tell me how?"

"The internet. Call me Bill, Gini."

"Verrdammt internet. Those papers were top secret and were supposed to be sealed away forever."

"The history of about the 10th was recently declassified and made public domain. They were buried deep in an electronic hole but I followed a trail until I fell upon them. They were in code. I guess the army figured no one would bother with them. I cracked the code...it was real simple."

"So Mr. Muntean..."

"Ut, ut, ut...call me Bill."

"So Bill, what do you want from me?"

"The truth Gini. Who were the American Bomber Girls? What is their story? Out of the 25,000 women who volunteered to fly combat, you and 1000 others were selected. I want to know the real story..."

"So you can write it for your own personal gain..."

"No Gini, because the world should know about the sacrifice made by of a group of American women during the war." Virginia was silent, and was sort of lost in thought. "It made sense you know," I continued, "A crew of women could carry much more fuel or bombs than a crew of men...making the women much more dangerous."

Once again Virginia was silent. Then she said, "The women carried something much more deadlier than bombs."

CHAPTER 9

THE BEGINNING

"What is it that you want to know?" asked Virginia.

"We could start at the beginning. You were 14 years old when you enlisted. Why did you join up? You were just a child. You should have been home doing all the things a 14 year old girl should have been doing in 1942."

"I have…I had two sisters who were much older than me. In the days after Pearl everyone wanted to do their patriotic duty and join the army to kill Japs. Then the next day Adolph declared war on the US. You know the United States was the only country that Hitler actually declared war on?"

"No, I did not know that," I admitted.

"So anyhow, my sisters were 19 and 17 years old and could enlist in the navy without parental consent. They both joined the WAVs. I made up my mind that there was no way, no way in hell I was going to stay home with my parents. We never had what you would call a good rapport my parents and me. I was always a bit of a rebel and that didn't sit well with my strict family. My father was old world like and lacked paternal instincts. Don't get me wrong, father was a good provider. During the Great Depression, my sisters and I never went without. However dad's only form of communication was with a strap or a belt. To make matters worse, he kept chickens, pigs and rabbits, not as pets, but as livestock and dad had no boys to help him out on his little farm. His main income came from working in a roller bearing mill in Canton, Ohio called Timken.

"So in late March, 1942, I found the courage to sneak out early one morning. I took some money out of my dad's wallet and then left a note for my mother. I only wished the letter could have said more.

"The bus stop was two miles from my house and I just barely got there with enough time to hop on. I took the bus to Canton and then went to the local recruitment center where I lied my ass off on the application. Back then there were no computers to verify your story and the army was desperate for warm bodies to replace cold ones so there were few questions asked. I was shipped out by noon that day."

The lady paused for a moment taking a deep breath before continuing, "I was put on another bus for a long trip to Ft. Des Moines in Des Moines, Iowa where I was scheduled to go through WAC boot camp. The bus trip was a grueling 24 hours long. We stopped at every damn little town along the way to pick up other enlistees and stretch. There were no other girls on the bus so all the boys wanted to sit next to me and talk. I ignored them because all I wanted was some peace and quiet. When I arrived at Ft. Des Moines, I found out I could have taken a train.

"Anyhow, I have to admit that I was scared to death and began to think that leaving home was a bad idea. Far from home, not knowing anyone, I wondered if anyone could tell how frightened I was. My hand was shaking when I filled out the registration card at the Fort. The Sergeant behind the counter where we dropped off the cards quickly stopped me. I thought the jig was already up," explain Ms. Morgenstern.

"Auxiliary White," said the Sergeant, "You did not leave a contact number."

"I don't have one, Sergeant," replied Virginia White.

"No next of kin either?"

"No Sergeant," said the petit 14 year old girl quietly shaking her head.

"None at all?"

"No Sergeant."

"So be it. Move along."

"Yes Sergeant." *'That was close,'* Virginia thought to herself.

The first day was consumed by the arrival of all the recruits and registrations, a quick physical examination and blood typing, AB Negative. The day was capped off by dinner in the mess hall. In all the excitement, Virginia did not realize how hungry she was. There was little to eat on the bus ride, no Wendy's or Burger Kings in 1942, and she was so nervous she could not think about eating anyway.

As she filled her tray, Virginia relaxed some feeling the worst was over. She sat alone at a table but was soon surrounded by a group of girls who had already met on the train ride to the Fort. They talked amongst themselves before one spoke with Virginia.

"Hello," said one of the girls, "You look like you just got out of kindergarten let alone old enough to be a WAC."

"I'm old enough," said Virginia defensively. After all she was small compared to most of the girls, only 5'5", her short blond hair was filthy dirty and flowed from under a Cleveland Indians baseball cap that she wore backwards. Virginia tanned well in the warm Ohio summers. Her European skin allowed her to keep her color through out the winter, unlike most northerners, so she had a brown complexion.

"Don't get all huffy, just saying hello little girl," said the lady.

"Sorry…my name is Gini. I just stepped off a 24 hour bus ride and I'm a little rattled by all this. The hell, I've never been more than 60 miles from my home in 18 years."

"Honey you are not 18 years old. But don't worry; your secret is safe with us. I'm Sally, from Chicago. It was a quick train ride here for me. This is Gina, that is Monica and that is Terry Lee."

"How ya doin'," said Terry Lee with a southern draw.

"Where are you from, Terry?" asked Virginia.

"I'm from the great state of Tennessee. I have to say that gitin' used to you Yankees is gonna take some doin'," said Terry.

"You have pigs in your yard, Terry Lee?" asked Virginia.

"Yeah, what of it," replied Terry ready for a fight.

"So do I. So you see we are not so different," said Virginia.

They all laughed. "Reckon not Gini…you're alright," said Terry Lee.

After dinner, the women were shown to their bunks in a large plywood building that once housed horses when the Calvary trained at Ft. Des Moines. Virginia fell right to sleep. She had only cat napped in the last 32 hours so she was exhausted.

¥

Reveille came quickly at 6 AM the next morning. "C'mon Gini get up. We only have 15 minutes to get dressed and the Sergeant will be here any second," said Terry Lee attempting to rouse Virginia.

"Go away! Wake me after the war," said Virginia turning on her side away from Terry.

"You leave me with no choice Yank." Terry lifted Virginia's mattress with her on it dumping the slumbering slug on the floor. "The south has risen…so should you." With a rebel yell Terry danced over Virginia's sprawled body lying on the floor.

Virginia managed to get organized. She fell out with the other women, and then dressed right before their Sergeant arrived and began blowing her whistle as if she needed anymore attention than she demanded the moment the older women appeared. Their Sergeant, Ms. Ramsey, explained the schedule for the day.

After a decent breakfast, the recruits were back at the barracks putting things in order… the military way. Sergeant Ramsey demonstrated the correct way to make a bed with tight 'hospital' corners and flat sheets. She had to explain the process of bed making to a few of the girls over again much to Terry's delight.

"Dumb Yankees," she commented and she and Virginia chuckled.

"Auxiliary Lee, Auxiliary White, do you find something amusing?" asked the Sergeant.

"Not any more, Sergeant," said Virginia.

"I'm from New York and a big Yankee fan. Drop and give me 10."

Virginia got into her billfold. "I only got a five dollar bill Sergeant. Can I owe you the rest?" she said in all honesty.

Sergeant Ramsey rolled her eyes with a heavy sigh. "Drop and give me ten push ups, White."

"Oh, sorry Sergeant. You should have said that," said Virginia.

"You will give me ten push ups with every wise crack. Am I clear, Auxiliary?"

"Crystal, Sergeant."

"You say 'Yes Sergeant'. Am I clear?"

"Yes…I get it," replied Virginia trying to be polite.

Ramsey shook her head and then returned to where she left off explaining procedures to the girls.

Once the barracks were in order, the girls went to another depot to receive their uniforms. Pants, shirts, ties, caps, jackets and even some cosmetics because the Army wanted the WACs to maintain their femininity. Sergeant Ramsey instructed the ladies on how to dress the Army way and how to wear their uniform. Blouses buttoned, hair off the collar, tie straight, hat on right and shoes shined.

"Everyone assembled on the parade grounds on the double," ordered Ramsey. The recruits were all quick to convene however Terry and Virginia straggled behind. Auxiliary White and Lee, nice of you to join us. Where have you been?"

"We got loss," said Virginia with all honesty.

"You got lost. Drop and give me ten."

"What the hell for?" protested Virginia.

"Make it 20. The rest of you form four rows of ten."

When Virginia was finished, Sergeant Ramsey demonstrated the maneuvers in a close order drill. "Now you try it," she said. "Right face!" Only half of the ladies turned right, the others turned left. "Eyes front." Everyone was facing Ramsey again. "Let's try this again. LEFT FACE." That time they all got it right.

Ramsey gave them a few more commands while they were in formation. The girls performed reasonably well. "Ok. This time we are going to march in order. Start with your left foot. I'll give you a moment to figure out your left from your right. When I say forward march, you will step with your left foot in unison. When I say left face, you turn left. Got it? Alright, forward march."

The women were understandably nervous after all how many people have ever marched before? They all started out ok until Sally fell out of step. She scuffled her feet so she was back in the rhythm but dropped out of step again and did the shuffle thing again. She became very distracting.

Ramsey didn't notice Sally. "Left, Right, left, right," she droned on.

Terry accidently stepped on Monica's heel causing her to yelp and stumble into the girl in front of her who was looking down at her feet. She then fell in front of Gina who tripped and fell in front of her whole row.

"HALT!" shouted Ramsey. She stared at the messy clumsy pile of uniformed ladies sitting on the pavement and with Virginia towering over them. Virginia just shrugged and did a sort of twist dance. "You girls are really PISSING ME OFF!" shouted Ramsey. "White, give me ten."

"What did I do?"

"You're a smart ass. And something tells me you were in the middle of this train wreck. Alright everyone on your feet we are going to do this again. If any of you want dinner tonight you had best get this right because we are staying out here 'til you do."

By dinner time on that first day of marching the ladies were too tired to eat. Virginia choked down a nice steak and mash potatoes. All the recruits wanted to do was just hit the hay.

¥

Reveille came quickly at 6 AM the next morning. "C'mon Virginia get up. We only have 15 minutes to get dressed and the Sergeant will be here any second," said Terry attempting to rouse Virginia.

"Go away. Wake me after the war," said Virginia turning on her side away from Terry.

"You leave me with no choice Yank." Terry lifted Virginia's mattress with her on it dumping the slumbering slug on the floor. "The south has risen…so should you." With a rebel yell Terry danced over Virginia lying on the floor.

"I'm experiencing déjà vu," Virginia said aloud while sitting cross legged on the floor nodding her head. She managed to pull herself together and dressed right with the others in time.

"Alright ladies you have 15 minutes to go inside and change into your shorts and tees. We are going to get some exercise this morning," said Ramsey.

Des Moines at the end of March was not exactly balmy. The ladies collected at the athletic field. They huddled together shivering. "Alright girls 10 laps around the football field…that will warm you up," said Ramsey.

Virginia did well. She always had to walk or sometimes run to the bus stop at home being that she lived so far from town. The girl led the rest of the pack by the first turn with Terry right behind her.

"I'm breathing down your neck, Yank," said Terry.

"I know Reb, I can hear your two lead feet," responded Virginia.

Virginia left the other girls behind but felt the taller stronger Tennessean ever on her back as the recruits circled the football field. When the duo rounded the last turn, Terry attempted to pass Virginia. Terry's attempt served to be futile because Virginia sped up staying just ahead of Terry.

Ramsey had never seen two recruits racing to be first in the class. They all knew where the finish line was because 'Finish' was painted on the paved track. They had already passed it nine times. As they approached the finish line Terry began to slow, Virginia finished well ahead of her before tumbling in the cold wet grass gasping for her next breath. Terry collapsed next to her also looking for a bite of air.

Virginia was smiling at Terry who was sitting on the wet ground with her head between her knees gasping. "The south has fallen again…better luck next time, Reb," said the Ohio girl before shoving the southern belle into the grass with her knee and then dancing off.

"Yeah, next time Yank," said Terry slowly rising to her feet.

"Alright ladies," said Ramsey, "form ranks in the middle of the field for jumping jacks."

The calisthenics lasted for two hours before breakfast. The ladies did well however they were required to do three chin ups to graduate. Two girls had to lift Virginia just so she could reach the bar.

CHAPTER 10

THE CO-PILOT OF 'THE ANGRY ALBATROSS'

At the age of 29, Lieutenant Kelli Blankenship was much older than most of the American Bomber Girls with the exception of her Captain Jennifer Edwards. Born in the Chicago area, her father would take Kelli on Sunday picnics at a small airfield on the edge of town that is now called Midway International Airport. She was the oldest of four children and the only girl in the family. Ironically, her brothers did not share their sister's and father's interest in airplanes or flying so they stayed home. Ergo Kelli and her dad picnicked at the airfield just to watch the Curtiss JN-4 Jenny biplanes take off, fly around and land.

JN-4 Jenny

When Kelli was nine, in 1922, she accompanied her father to a large air show at the Checkerboard Field outside of Chicago. In addition to the WW I fighters and bombers on display, there were all types of talented pilots performing a variety of dare devil stunts in their JN-4 Jenny's. The flyers did loop-the-loops, barrel rolls, figure 8's, wing walking and the most daring of their stunts, killing the engine at a high altitude, free falling and then starting the engine just before becoming a part of the pavement. These pilots were called 'barnstormers'.

Barnstormers in the 20s were usually former WW I pilots (American and some from Europe) who traveled across the country performing fantastic stunts for crowds in small towns. Some travelled together in small groups calling themselves a flying circus. Most were simply individuals who made living doing a few air acrobatics followed by charging the spectators for rides in their amazing flying machines.

Bessie Coleman

Performing at the Checkerboard Field air show was the world's first black aviatrix named Bessie Coleman. Ms. Coleman was born with three drawbacks that prevented her fulfilling her dream of being a pilot. The first was that she was a woman; the second was that she was Black and the third was that she was an American. While being a manicurist at a barber shop near the Chicago field, she heard the stories the WW I flyers told about their days during the war. That was when Ms. Coleman decided she wanted to learn to fly.

No American flight school would enroll a woman, let alone a woman of color, so Ms. Coleman raised the money needed to go to Paris and learn to fly. In six months she became the first black woman with not only a pilot's license but an international license. She came back to the US but found the only way to make money flying was to be a barnstormer. Ms. Coleman wanted to learn more advanced flying skills and some more tricky maneuvers. She was once again not accepted to any flight school in the US.

Ms. Coleman returned to France in 1922 to improve her flying skills. While in Europe, she met Anthony Fokker of the Netherlands. Fokker was an aviation designer and engineer and also the founder of the Fokker Corporation a leading company in aeronautics. Ms. Coleman joined Fokker in the Netherlands where his best pilots instructed her on how to really fly. Ms. Coleman returned to the United States and started making a good income barnstorming.

Kelli Blankenship's father gave Kelli the money needed to go for a plane ride with, by that time, the famous aviatrix. Before Kelli climbed into the JN-4, she and Ms. Coleman exchanged a few words. Kelli's father observed the conversation and was about to intervene when for some reason he watched Ms. Coleman put the 9 year old girl into the front cockpit which was usually reserved for the pilot and Ms. Coleman climbed in the cockpit behind the pilot which had the same controls as the pilot seat, just no instruments.

After being airborne for 10 minutes, Ms. Coleman relinquished the controls to Kelli. They flew level for a few minutes before Ms. Coleman instructed the young girl on how to turn, accelerate and climb. Kelli did very well. The duo flew around longer than most. Kelli really got the hang of piloting.

So anyhow, the plane ride lasted 25 minutes but would affect Kelli for a lifetime. From then on, Kelli could not be bothered by the things that bothered nine year old girls in the 1920s. She built a mock-up of the cockpit of a JN-4 out of cardboard in her bed room. Her plane was complete with a rudder, steering column and operating flaps. Her father was proud of his little girl but Kelli was not permitted to enroll in flight school until she was 15 and a half years old. At the age of 16, she was the second youngest female to earn her wings.

Kelli's father bought her an aging, beat JN-4 that leaked oil and gas and would not run unless it belched huge clouds of smoke. Father was a top notch mechanic and had no trouble at all rebuilding the plane's engine so it ran like new. Kelli flew the plane on week ends during high school and gave rides to those who had a few bucks. The money chiefly went towards fuel and maintenance.

By the time Kelli graduated high school she had developed into a very beautiful lady…a solid dime. She was tall, nearly six feet, with long wavy golden rod colored hair that flowed down past her broad shoulders to her hour glass figure and perfectly proportioned hips. The girl had little interest in romantic relationships. If a man became serious about Kelli he would always take the same old stand and say 'No wife of mine was going to spend her days flying around the countryside. She's gonna stay home and raise the kids…' a real deal breaker for Kelli.

Then came the Great Depression and it looked as if Kelli would be grounded by the lack of money for gas. Fortunately, she found a want-ad for a pilot in a flyer's trade magazine. In 1933, she was quickly employed by a wealthy business man who flew the country buying large estates from those less fortunate who lost everything in the stock market. The guy would pick up acres for pennies on the dollar. He hired Kelli for her flying abilities too, but mostly because of her good looks. The sleaze bag had a female pilot and crew and always insisted they unbutton their shirts in the air. Actually, this scum bag was refreshing after the a-holes Kelli had to deal with at home.

The young aviatrix was doing well, travelling the country, pulling in big bucks and dodging advances from the boss. She flew his Lockheed Electra for 10 years and for 10 years she told her boss that if he were the last man on Earth she would douse him with gasoline and burn him alive. Kelli was still in his service after Pearl Harbor. She considered joining the WASPs but her boss gave her a big fat bonus to keep flying for him.

One day the unthinkable happened. Kelli was at the controls when her vision blurred and went dark. She fell back in her seat before throwing up. Fortunately the plane was equipped with a new gadget called 'autopilot'.

The co-pilot landed the plane in Chicago and Kelli's parents rushed her to the hospital.

When she woke up two days later, she was told she had a disease of which there was no treatment. She was also informed that her pilot's license was revoked. In addition, there was a mysterious uniformed man waiting to see her.

CHAPTER 11

BOOT CAMP

For the first time, Virginia was up and organized sans Terry Lee's assistance. Following breakfast, the women were introduced to their school work. For the first two weeks of their four week stay at Ft. Des Moines, the recruits became accustomed to the military way of life. The mornings were spent in class rooms. They were educated on military protocol and courtesies such as how to address officers. In addition, the women were taught current events, Army hygiene, arithmetic, map reading, airplane identification and many other useful skills that would serve them in their new career in the military.

After lunch there was marching, hours and hours and hours and hours and hours and hours and hours and hours and hours and hours and hours and hours of marching. The girls marched everywhere. In less than one week the clumsy collection of recruits stayed in step and looked liked a well choreographed dance troop. When the girls were not marching there was exercise, always exercise. Later the obstacle course was introduced complete with a seven foot wall that the girls had to clear on their own without any help. Then there was still the 'three chin ups or you're out' rule.

The few hours after dinner were spent in study hall after which the ladies were permitted some free time for themselves. Some would have a cola while participating in a competitive yet friendly game of ping pong. Some reviewed the day's school work while others were satisfied just to kick back and talk with the other women in their unit until lights out at 10 pm.

Boot camp was a cinch for Virginia. She was accustomed to being ordered about by a stern father so Sergeant Ramsey was not much of a change. The classes were easy for her. The girls in the 1930s who did go on to high school were taught the important subjects that a good mother or housewife needed to know. They took classes in cooking, sewing and that sort of thing. Not much arithmetic. Teaching mathematics to a house wife was seen as a gross waste of time.

Virginia liked arithmetic and was damn good at it. She could look at an equation and the answer would just appear in her head. In Ohio, her abilities were not appreciated and in some cases frowned upon. The Ohio way. The lack of a well rounded education was unfortunate for many of the women who needed to study extra hard to pass their exams. For if a recruit did not do well, they had to quit or were asked to resign.

Sally was able to run the obstacle course, scaled the seven foot wall and finish with a good time. She had no trouble doing the three chin ups. That was all fine but the girl had next to no education in arithmetic besides the basic adding and subtracting. In addition, she had no training in science.

So, while on the athletic field, Sergeant Ramsey ordered the unit to do 10 laps around the field. Virginia saw no need to work hard so she maintained a steady pace just ahead of the pack. Sally had to demonstrate her maximum effort to catch up to her. "Gini," Sally puffed, "will you…slow down…for a moment?"

Virginia accommodated her class mate, "What's up Sally?"

"Please don't be offended but I need a favor."

"Sure Sally, what can I do for you?"

"I don't want to be sent home. Will you help me with the arithmetic, I just can't get it?"

"Yeah, I'll help you with the arithmetic on one condition."

"Name it!"

"Help me with those damnable three chin ups."

"It's a deal, Gini."

Then there was that damn whistle, "White, Thompson, you're doggin' it," said Ramsey.

¥

That night, lights out was at 10 PM as usual. Normally Virginia fell right to sleep and did not wake before reveille but that night something was keeping her up. Maybe it was the excitement of being away from home and making new friends. Or it was the fear of being drummed out of the WAC's and having to go home and explain herself to her nutty father. That would keep anyone up. She was not certain exactly what was keeping her awake but her tossing and turning accompanied by her repeated heavy sighs served to disturb Terry Lee in the rack next to hers.

"What's bothering you, Yank?" asked Terry in a whisper so not to disturb the rest of the barracks.

"I don't know!" said Virginia with one more sigh. "Why did you join the Army, Terry?"

"I joined because my brother was killed at Pearl. He was just 18 proud, brave and serving on the 'Arizona'.

As far as we know, he went down with his ship. I want some payback. I hope to be assigned to the Pacific."

"Why didn't join the WAVs?"

"Shoo, I'm not going to give the Navy a chance to kill another Lee. No, I'll do fine in the Army. Besides, I liked the idea of gittin' out of Tennessee for a spell. I've done just about all there is to do in my little town. How about you? What are you doing here?"

"I dreaded the idea of being home alone with my parents after my two sisters joined the WAVs."

"What's the mater? Isn't Ohio a fun place?"

"Weeeeeeell, no. Not at all," said Virginia shaking her head. "It's always cold and the air is smelly. My parents and I never had what you would call a close relationship. My fondest memory is spending time with my grandfather." Virginia shifted on her side facing Terry, "We would go to Cleveland to see the Indians play baseball. It was an all day affair. Granddad bought me a beer."

"Your grandfather drank with you and no one said anything?"

"Nope, I guess everybody thought he was my dad and if your dad gives you a beer...it's ok. We would drink what they called pounders because the cups were 16 ounces. I would have two sometimes three pounders."

"Just between the two of us...how old are you?" asked Terry.

"I'm 18, Terry."

"Ya gonna still sing that tired old tune. Ok, you're 18. What would bring you closer to your dad, Gini?"

"My dad said I'd never amount to much. He would be proud of me if I were raped and murdered by the Japanese. The worst thing about living in Ohio was that I never felt I belonged there. I had a few friends but I was always different. I felt I should be out there exploring new lands…looking for the Emerald City. Do you ever feel that way Terry?" The girl in the bed next to her did not respond but Virginia could hear her snoring. "I always like to keep my audience captivated," said Virginia.

¥

For two weeks, every day consisted of marching, calisthenics and classes, marching, calisthenics and classes, marching, calisthenics and classes, marching, calisthenics and of course classes. At the end of the two weeks, there were tests to see if the recruits learned anything. Sergeant Ramsey handed out Certificate of Achievement for those who passed. All the remaining girls in the unit successfully moved on. Virginia did her trade mark little dance when she accepted the parchment.

"You still gotta do those chin ups White," said Ramsey. Virginia did not say a word but returned a snappy salute.

The recruits were moved from the stables to Boom Town a collection of brand new red brick buildings that were more comfortable. In addition, they were assigned to their specialized fields. Ramsey read off their assignment, "Gina Emerson, secretary, Monica Smith, nursing, Sally Young, transport, Terry Lee, radio operations,"

"Yes!" said Terry.

"Virginia White, building maintenance."

"What!!??" objected Virginia.

"Problem White."

"No Sergeant," said Virginia with a sigh.

The last weeks Virginia plunged toilets, fixed locks, patched dry wall, hung ceiling fans and did small repairs around the base. One day a Colonel asked (ordered the auxiliary), to assist him in planning a new kitchen to be installed in a barrack for the Officers. "We are going to put tile on these walls Auxiliary. The tile comes in 17 inch pieces. Write this down," ordered the Colonel as he did a quick calculation on his slide rule. (A primitive calculating device before calculators. A tad bit more advanced than an abacus.)

"So with the trimmed pieces we will need ten pieces to do a wall. Write that down."

"Begging your pardon Colonel," interjected Virginia, "You will need eight pieces. Your error is that you multiplied the trim pieces by 1.6 when you should have used 1.67. Taking your factor to the 100's made a big difference."

The Colonel looked at the petit girl about half his size. After taking a few minutes to physically measure the wall with a ruler and record his finding, he took a deep breath. "Looks like you are right, Auxiliary. You did that in your head, did you?"

Virginia shrugged, "Yes Sir. I'm Virginia White, Auxiliary,15316101."

"Auxiliary White, that wall is 260 square feet and we get 400 square feet out of one gallon of paint. How many gallons do we need and still have a gallon left over?"

"Seven will do it," said Virginia with little hesitation.

The Colonel did the calculation on his slide rule and then shook his head in disbelief. "You're right again. Ms. White I'm Colonel Williams. Come with me."

CHAPTER 12

THE BOMBARDIER & TOP TURRET GUNNER OF 'THE ANGRY ALBATROSS'

Rules are made to be broken. Marie Trembley was Canadian. Her father was French and mother was Canadian Indian of the Cree tribe. Ever since Marie was born, she had a severe wander lust. Fortunately, the US entered the war right after her 17th birthday and high school graduation. Marie felt that Canada was too far from the action at the front so she applied and was quickly accepted into the British ATA.

Rules are made to be broken. Marie was not tall enough to be an A-TA-girl. She was 5 foot when the rules called for 5'7" or better. Second, she lied about having a pilot's license and stated on her application she had sufficient hours to qualify for the ATA. She had planed on learning enough about flying a plane before she needed to take the controls of a warbird. The reason for her snappy acceptance into the ATA was that she spoke English and French well. In addition, while taking the entrance exam, she finished all the math on the test including the advanced Calculus while the other girls were struggling with multiplication.

Math came easy; actually school was easy for a girl with an I. Q. of 157. Marie was also easy going and a joy to talk with. She was pretty, petit, with long black stick-straight hair that hung down pass her shoulders. Her dark brown eyes were supported by a pair of high check bones that produced little dimples when she smiled.

To remedy the whole no pilot's license problem, Marie would sneak off alone and use her photographic memory to study flying. Her plan didn't work. The first time she was behind the controls of a plane, she missed half the check list. While taxiing down the runway, her instructor politely asked her to stop the plane. "Have you ever flown a plane before, Marie?" he asked. The jig was up.

It seemed that the ATA was not the only organization to note Marie's Mathematical talents. Two days later while she was packing to return to Canada, she was informed that a mysterious uniformed man was waiting to see her in the Generals office.

¥

Sandy O'Malley was a dead shot. Her Irish father gave Sandy a loaded .22 caliber rifle on her 5th birthday in 1924 and taught her how to shoot it. He was a veteran from the First World War and saw some action in France. The Army gave him a gun and taught him how to use it. From then on he was hooked. He became a gun enthusiast. Upon returning to the US, after WW I, he met and married Sandy's Swedish mother. Sandy was born nine months later in 1919.

Sandy entered and won many shooting competitions in her home state of Minnesota, most of the time against men and boys much older than herself. She had so many victories that her father converted the den into a room full of Sandy's trophies and ribbons all before her 12th birthday. In addition, there were numerous newspaper and magazine articles about Sandy neatly framed and hung on the wall with her awards. She became a member of the National Rifle Association (NRA was established in 1871) at the age of 13. At home, Sandy was recognized as the best skeet shooter and a fine hunter.

Just prior to her 18th birthday, 1936, Sandy joined the WACs. There was rumbling in Europe once again and if war was to break out, Sandy wanted to be in on it. WACs were not supposed to have a gun but while watching a men's unit practice shooting at targets, Sandy strolled onto the firing line, found a loaded Springfield M 1 Grand field rifle and starting popping off at a distant target clearly without permission. The Master Sergeant in charge had a fit until he saw her target. Sandy fired ten times but there were only three holes…she hit the same hole numerous times. She went on to receive all the Army Marksmanship badges and all medals available.

The year 1939 proved to be a bad year for all concern. Hitler invaded Poland and then Sandy's life took a nasty careen downward. Her father was accidently killed in a hunting accident. Sandy was heart broken. She received a 30 day pass 29 of which she spent in bed sobbing. She tore the marksmanship badges from her WAC uniform and the proceeded to take all her trophies, ribbons and awards and threw them into the trash. Sandy swore to never pick up a rifle ever again.

Sandy returned to her position with the WACs as a radio operator at Ft. Ord. She figured hard work would make her feel better. She was invited to marksman competitions but she kept her vow and turned down the invites without any remorse. In December of 1940, just before Christmas Sandy was dealt a final blow…while marching with her unit, she had a heart attack and collapsed…at the young age of 21.

The following year was just hell for the girl. She did get out of bed and move about much. The doctors told her not to over exert herself. In June of 1941, the Germans invaded Russia. Sandy was not concerned with the world affairs however she did see an article in a 'Life Magazine' about a Russian woman. Sandy was impressed by Lyudmila Pavlicenko, a 24 year old Russian sniper.

Lyudmila Pavlicenko (18)

In 1941, 2000 Russian girls enlisted in the Soviet sniper school of which about 500 survived the war. The article was just a short blurb about Russian girls being snipers. Lyudmila Pavlicenko was the most successful female sniper in history and is still regarded as a top sniper today credited with 309 kills. Her nick name was 'Lady Death'.

Sandy managed to do more active things without any further incident. One day, while she was working in the family garden, she watched a military staff car pull up in front of her house. Out stepped a mysterious uniformed man who offered Sandy a chance to save the world while being in constant danger and not knowing at breakfast whether she would see dinner. Sandy agreed to his terms.

CHAPTER 13

VIRGINIA WHITE

Colonel Williams ordered Virginia to accompany him. "Colonel, Sergeant Ramsey told me to stay here," said Virginia.

"Ms. White, my bird does not take orders from stripes."

Virginia followed the Colonel across the parade grounds to a lone stone building. When they went inside the eyes of five men immediately transfixed on the auxiliary as they quickly came to attention. "Please, at ease men. Ms. White, this office is designed to calculate new air routes that will crisscross the US. These air routes will eventually be used to fly military aircraft from the factories to their point of debarkation to Europe. We calculate many variables here. Weather of course, up drafts down drafts coming off the mountains and large lakes. It is very involved and very secret. You may only work on one small part of the country so you never know the whole route. You can not speak about what you do here. Should anyone demand to know what you are doing, you just call me…I'll deal with them. Do you understand, Virginia?"

"Affirmative Sir!"

"Good. The boys here will get you acquainted with your duties. Boys you have a live one here. Treat her well…understand?"

"Yes sir!" they all said in unison.

¥

Virginia was late for chow that evening and was met by a most hostile Sergeant who did not have an issue with giving Virginia a dressing down before the whole unit. "Auxiliary, were have you been? When I went to check on you and could not find you! I should send you home right this minute!"

"Sergeant, I was with Colonel Williams. He said if I have any trouble with anyone to call him right away and you…you…are…trouble. If you excuse me I'll call the Colonel and you can speak to him," said Virginia before calmly turning her back on Ramsey, casually strolling to the telephone on the reception desk and began dialing the Colonel's phone number.

"Auxiliary White!" shouted Ramsey with the eyes of the entire unit on her. Virginia ignored her Sergeant and listened to phone on the other end of the line begin to ring. "Auxiliary White!" shouted Ramsey again. Ramsey quickly walked over to Virginia and pressed down the phone disconnecting the call. "That won't be necessary. I'm going to check on your story in the morning. If you are lying to me…I'll hang your corpse on the parade grounds, understand?"

"As you wish, Sergeant."

CHAPTER 14

THE PILOT OF 'THE ANGRY ALBATROSS'

Jennifer Edwards was just barely eking out a living as a self-proclaimed barnstormer during the Great Depression. The aviatrix travelled across the Northeastern United States in the summer and then the Southern states in the winter months performing her awe-inspiring brand of stunts for amazed crowds. Following her shows, she would give rides to anyone who could scrape together a few bucks. Most of the money she made went towards gas, engine maintenance and food. The girl spent her nights camped out in a field somewhere with her JN-4 Jenny on the left side and a loaded .45 on the right.

There were not many barnstormers left in the depression. The Department of Commerce passed a bunch of 'safety' laws against flying too low and having people walking on wings and such. Those new laws severely limited the barnstormer's shows and stunts. To avoid constant fines, and because they could not meet payroll, the flying circuses all disbanded. The solo barnstormers did not make the money they did before the stock market crashed so they all took straight jobs…sometimes out of the cockpit. Jennifer OWNED the skies. She dodged the US Government and continued to do the breath taking stunts the barnstormers were known for. Most times when she flew over a town, it was the first time many had ever seen an airplane and clambered to be first to fly in one. Jennifer was doing OK.

Despite the lack of disposable income, Jennifer would not trade her life for anyone's. Free to travel the country, work when she wanted or do nothing iffen she felt like it. She loved to fly and was more comfortable alone in the sky then anywhere else. Sometimes, Jennifer would climb into the heavens as high as her small plane would take her. Up there alone was cold; however, she said there was music playing and she could hear it. (I'm not making that up) Back on the ground, when life became too overwhelming, there was always the option of landing at her family farm for a respite, a bath, a hot meal and a warm bed.

The family farm, where Jennifer spent her whole life, was in Somerville, South Carolina, just outside of Charleston. It had been in the family's name for eight generations, since before the Revolutionary War thus there was no mortgage...only taxes. Mr. Edwards was brilliant. He raised enough money from crops to feed Jennifer's five brothers and sisters with plenty left over to sell to large corporations. In addition, no one in the town of Somerville went hungry...not as long as Mr. Edwards was there. After the Great War, when JN-4's were offered for sale by the military for $200, (they cost the US $5500) Mr. Edwards managed to secure one for his favorite daughter. Don't tell anyone Jennifer was his favorite. It was her dad's secret.

Jennifer began flying at the age of 17. She grew into a tall slender woman with long brown hair. Unlike most ladies, she was very plain but beautiful with green eyes, a small pug nose and a bright smile. During the summer following high school graduation in 1934 and after her 18th birthday, Jennifer was at an air show in Charleston, South Carolina where she saw part-time barnstormer Clyde Pangborn do his famous stunt, walking across the wing of his plane on to the wing of another. Jennifer was impressed with Pangborn who was 40 years old at that time. She met him after the show and insisted he teach her some skilled flying maneuvers. Pangborn was a successful pilot and barnstormer during the heydays of the 20s. He was part owner of the Gates Flying Circus which was one of the companies that ended in 1929. After the company collapse, he still maintained a successful career flying periodically returning to his roots as a barnstormer.

Pangborn took an immediate liking to Jennifer, took her under his wing…sorta speak…and taught her stunt flying. The duo partnered up for a period of time barnstorming across northern United States. Jennifer was a quick study and learned her trade well. Pangborn had other interests so Jennifer flew on her own most of the time. Once in awhile they would do a show together but Pangborn then had to move on.

In 1941, Jennifer was performing a loop-the-loop when she made a quick emergency landing in a corn field. When the crowd gathered around her plane, they found the aviatrix unconscious and draped over the controls of the aircraft. She had elapses such that one before but was always alone and on the ground when they happened so the aviatrix kept the incidents to herself. When Jennifer woke up three days later, she was informed that there was a terminal illness in her brain and nothing could be done for her.

Jennifer flew back to the family farm to find a letter from the Department of Commerce notifying her that her pilot's license was revoked. Mr. Edwards sold the JN-4…no sense keeping it. After all the blows life had dealt the young woman, watching her beloved plane fly away was the worst. She spent the next year rattling around the old house and farm or lying in bed for days due to depression. Her mother could not look at Jennifer without bursting into tears. Fortunately for Jennifer, the Japs bombed Pearl Harbor. A few months later a USAAF staff car rolled up to the door of the farm house and a mysterios uniformed man stepped out looking for Jennifer Edwards.

CHAPTER 15

VIRGINIA GRADUATES

The second two weeks simply flew by. Virginia did her chin ups with Sally's coaching. Finally it was graduation day. Before the ceremony, Sergeant Ramsey handed out their assigned posts.

"Gina Emerson: Ft. Benning, Georgia. Monica Smith: Ft. Hood, Texas, Terry Lee: Ft. Ord, California. Looks like you may get your wish, Lee. A few WACs disembarked for the Orient from Ft. Ord.

"Auxiliary White," Ramsey froze, "This has got to be a misprint. I can't believe my eyes. Someone else has to read this, I SIMPLY CAN'T DO IT!!"

Sally took the papers from Ramsey and then her jaw fell to the floor. "It says here, 'Corporal Virginia White will report to the United States Army Air Base at New Castle, Rhode Island.'" Sally smiled at Virginia, "No shit Gini, I mean Corporal White, that's what it says." Then Sally snapped off a salute to Virginia.

"God bless America, the whole world has gone nuts!" shouted Ramsey. "This is one crazy ass war. The hell, we may win it anyhow." Ramsey reached into a locker and produced a WAC Corporal's uniform. "I was afraid they sent this for me. You'd best get dressed White…I mean Corporal, commencement is starting shortly." Ramsey saluted Virginia before taking her leave. The

WACs gathered around Virginia to congratulate her with pats on the head and shoulders and hugs.

Their unit joined several other WAC units graduating that day. There was marching, of course, while a brass band played the best of John Philip Sousa. The graduates took their seats to listen to a few speeches. After which they were dismissed to celebrate.

¥

Virginia arrived at New Castle Air Base following a long but comfortable train ride. Upon arrival at the train station, a woman in a Lieutenant uniform, along with two enlisted men, was waiting on the platform. "This way Corporal," said the tall chubby red haired Lieutenant the moment Virginia stepped out of the club car carrying only her duffle bag. The Lieutenant was not a WAC, but was dressed in a USAAF uniform with an officer's cap.

"Miss White I am in charge of the unit you have been assigned. My name is Lieutenant Zoë Cole, but you can call me Zoë, our department is rather informal."

"Thank you Lieutenant Cole. Is that coal, like a lump of coal?" asked Virginia.

"No it is Cole as in Cole."

"We used coal to fire the furnace in the winter," said Virginia not trying to be a wise ass.

"No Corporal, my name is Cole."

They reached the end of the platform and climbed into Zoë's waiting JEEP. "I don't get it," said Virginia.

Zoë started the engine and put the vehicle into gear. "I don't know…they told me you were smart," she said shaking her head before roaring off.

When Virginia arrived at New Castle in the late spring of 1942, the base was still a year from being opened. Virginia's mission was to develop air routes for military planes across Europe much like what she had done at Ft. Des Moines. In addition to the small contingent of service personnel at New Castle, there was a group of WASPs stationed there.

The guard at the camp gate recognized Zoë so the two service women were waved through. Zoë showed Virginia around the small base before taking her to the office. New Castle was a long way from anywhere so it was its own self contained little city complete with a PX, barber shop and movie theatre. They eventually arrived at Cole's office. There were a dozen men looking at maps and doing calculations with pen and paper. They came to their feet when Zoë entered the room. "Gentlemen please return to what you were doing," said Zoë. "I hate it when they do that," she whispered to Virginia.

On the wall was a large map of the north coast of France, the coast of Germany and the English Channel. "Much of our work up until now has been designing air routes across the US," said Zoë. "Now, as you can see, we have a broader and more important job. You will be doing the same type of job you did in Des Moines, only now we will be designing air routes for our bombers to fly into Europe and out again safely. We need the planes to be able to fly further on the same amount of fuel."

"Oh...boy," said Virginia with a heavy sigh.

"I see you get the picture Gini," said Zoë. "I don't have to tell you that this job is classified top secret. You may never...I mean never, leave the base without two escorts. That goes for everyone not just because you are a woman. Come along Virginia, I'll show you to your quarters." Virginia did not hear Zoë's order. She stood there staring up at the big mapped wall wondering if she was going to be able to do the job. What were they going to say when they found out she couldn't? She shuddered. "Virginia come on," said Zoë more demanding.

"Oh, sorry Lieutenant," said Virginia.

Zoë showed Virginia to the mess hall and then to here own room with her on bath. "You can have the rest of the day off," said Zoë. "Dinner is at five. Take this time to get comfortable. In the morning, you will be in a meteorology class for a few days just to catch you up."

"Thank you, Lieutenant."

"Please, call me Zoë.

¥

Life at New Castle could not be much better. Virginia worked from eight in the morning until six in the afternoon. There were plenty of other women on the base and then there were the WASPs. Virginia envied the WASPs because they were able to go flying. Several times she sneaked on to one of the military planes with the WASP Captain's permission and spent the afternoon flying over Delaware. "Wouldn't you like to be flying bombing missions in the heavies?" the Captain would ask Virginia.

"What and be shot at by some German ace…no thanks. Sometimes I think how nuts those guys must be. I don't think I could do it," said Virginia.

On the weekends Virginia would go to the camp pub for a few beers with the other women. She would be hit on by Majors and Captains. Only 15 years old and being hit on. If those guys only knew how much trouble they would be in if Virginia said yes. She didn't go home with anyone of course.

Virginia's work troubled her. She and her crew were doing what they could to direct the heavy bombers to and from their targets, however; their losses kept increasing. 40% of the last bombing mission did not return. Sixty bombers took off and only 36 returned. Of the 36 that come back, three crashed upon landing and had to be scrapped out. The B-17s and the B-24s were well armed. Why were they being chopped up by the German Messerschmitt? Virginia would stand there and stare at the big board and wonder what she was missing.

Virginia was at New Castle for six months before her next promotion to Sergeant. Sometimes for relaxation Virginia would help out around the base doing odd jobs, some painting and things such as that. One afternoon, she was painting a room with one of an enlisted man who she actually had a thing for. They were having a good time talking and drinking a few beers that the boy slipped into the building they were working on. Virginia was up on a ladder telling her man about Ohio when she fell and smacked her head.

Virginia woke a day or so later in a hospital bed. She recollected painting and being on the ladder but nothing after that. Zoë was her first visitor and explained how she was in some deep trouble. "But Zoë, we didn't have very much to drink," Virginia admitted.

"You were drinking?" asked Zoë hearing this for the first time.

Virginia looked at her friend and boss, "Nooo," she lied. "How am I in trouble Zoë?'

"You have a rare blood disease. The doctors say there is nothing that can be done for you and that it is terminal.

You are going to get an honorable discharge, Virginia." Virginia was quiet with an empty expression on her face. "OH MY!!" cried Zoë. "You didn't know, did you? Oh Gini, I'm so sorry for blurting it out like that. I thought you knew," said Zoë giving Virginia a hug. Tears welled up in Zoë's eyes. "Virginia...I'm so sorry. You know you are going home?"

Again Virginia was quiet as she rolled on her side with her back towards Zoë. *'Going home..... what a horrible thought. Spending the rest of my short life dying...that is if my father doesn't kill me as soon as I walk in the door.'* Virginia went on inside her head, *'I can't go back to Canton, Ohio, and I'd rather die in a blazing B-17. I wonder if my dad would beat a Sergeant in the army.'* Virginia slipped off to sleep.

Virginia only slept for a few hours. When she woke it was in the middle of the afternoon. She turned on her back and focused on a uniformed man sitting in a chair along side her bed reading a book. "May I help you Colonel?" she asked.

"Ahhh good you're awake. How are you feeling Sergeant?"

"Pretty damn crappy. Thanks for askin'. You know I'm not a sergeant anymore. I'm being sent home."

"Is that what you want Ms. White?"

"I'm sorry...do I know you?"

"I'm Colonel George Daniels, USAAF. Do you want to go home Sergeant White?"

"No, Colonel, I do not!"

"Good! Ms. White, would you like to fly army aircraft?"

"Yeah, sure Colonel," said Virginia a bit bewildered.

"Well then, Ms. White, your country needs you."

"From Ohio?"

The Colonel chuckled. "Virginia, what I have to tell you is top secret. If you repeat it to anyone ever you can be charged with treason and face a firing squad. Do you understand?"

"Colonel, I have a very high clearance. There is little you can tell me I don't already know."

"Sergeant, I have put together a bomber squadron of all women."

Virginia shook her head, "You could tell me MOST anything…but I did not know that," she said a bit surprised.

"I have organized this concern with the approval of the United States Army Air Force and from General "Hap" Arnold himself. I'm offering you a job on an American bomber flying missions over Europe. You are already a good navigator and you understand Mathematics better than most. You will be a part of an air crew of all women including the ground crew and the mechanics."

Virginia slowly reached over her shoulder and pressed the button for the nurse. She felt that she would need help with this loon. "Go on," the girl in the bed politely said.

"I'm for real, Virginia. We are losing too many planes and men each day. We think that a small squadron of medium bombers can slip into enemy air space and slip out with few losses. In addition, the squadron would be protected by fighters. Light weight planes with a light weight crew can inflict more damage than the heavies. You can carry more fuel or more bombs than the men simply because the crew is smaller and lighter. You're supposed to be a smart girl, what do you think?"

"You want me to be a navigator?"

"That's all."

"Can I think about it?"

"Sure you can, Virginia. Think about it while you are lying in a bed dying in Ohio." Colonel Daniels was very frank with his candidates.

Virginia took a moment to think the offer through. Dying in Ohio or being shot down over Germany and burning to death. That definitely sounded better than Ohio. "Alright, I'm in. Where do we go from here?"

"You will join the WASP training at Avenger Field in Sweet Water, Texas. You need to learn how to navigate the Army way. One thing, Virginia, the most important thing, Virginia. This is all top secret. You can't tell anyone what you are doing."

"Since you put it that way, what can I say but don't you tell my parents.

CHAPTER 16

"THE ANGRY ALBATROS" FIRST MISSION

Beautiful mornings on an airfield have the potential to yield problems and or rare opportunities. Colonel Daniels of the USAAF and his all female squadron in training were stationed in Hardwick Air Force Base (AFB) in England. Daniels found out just how much trouble clear and sunny skies can cause a wing squadron Group Commander at 0630. A messenger summoned Daniels to the base General's office immediately.

"I'll be right there," responded the Colonel.

"The General insists that it is very urgent, Sir," said the messenger.

'What does that asshole want now?' pondered Colonel Daniels. Ever since he and the American Bomber Girls arrived at Hardwick AFB, 66 miles northwest of London, General James 'Jimmy' Thomas was a thorn in Daniels back side. "I'm on my way," said the Colonel.

Jimmy Thomas was described as the most annoying son-of-a-bitch in the whole army. History shows that he was only promoted by his commanding officers, not for his competency, but to move this pesty rash to someone else's office. The army stuck him in a backwater base call 'Hardwick' in charge of a squadron of women flyers in hopes he will not cause to much trouble.

"Morning General," said Daniels politely when he entered the Thomas's office.

"Sit down George," ordered the General. "There is no time to waste so I will come to the point...how quickly can you get your bomber group in the air on a vital mission?"

"They need a minimum of two weeks of training for bombing runs," replied Colonel Daniels.

"No George, how quick can we get them up this morning...more precisely, right now?"

"General, they have not flown even one practice bomb run. They have never had live ammo on their planes. We can't send them on a bomb run, against real fighters, they will get chopped to pieces. A men's group with limited training would not fare any better. It's suicide."

"Colonel, a group of RAF Lancasters were on their way back from a night time raid when they fell upon a wolf pack of 12 German submarines on the surface heading back to the submarine pens in Lorient, France. One of the Lancasters is still observing the subs. So far he has not been detected. George this is a great opportunity to send a dozen enemy subs to the bottom of the Atlantic."

"You want the 10th to fly the mission?"

"We have no one else. The Brits can't put together a flight fast enough. Our B-17's have already taken off on their mission before sunrise. I have already ordered the 10th fueled and armed. If the girls want to catch the subs without fighter protection, they have to leave in 45 minutes."

Colonel Daniels did not say anything, letting the idea of sending his women into combat so ill-prepared was nauseating. "This is insane," he said.

"Colonel Daniels," continued Thomas, "I have made it clear that I oppose this whole idea of women flying bombers. Hell most women aren't smart enough to mop floors let alone fly a bomber. In addition, I have objected to having women on my air base. Allow me to be blunt Colonel, if your 'American Bomber Girls' don't fly this mission and send those subs to Old Hobbs, they will be scrubbing toilets and taking dictation by noon today."

"You would never get away with that. General Arnold approved the formation of the 10th himself. He would never…"

"Hap and I both founded the 'Black Hand' at West Point. Whose side do you think he will take? You better get going Colonel. The longer you wait, the more fighters there will be."

Colonel Daniels stormed out of General Thomas's office quietly muttering something less than complimentary about Thomas and his mother's sex acts. He was met by his aide Major Margret Hayes.

"What are the women doing?" demanded Daniels.

"They had better be getting dressed and straightening up the barracks like I just ordered them to do, Colonel," replied Hayes.

"Change in orders…get them into their flight gear and in the briefing room in 10 minutes."

"Are they going on a surprise practice run?"

"It's a surprise alright…but it is not practice…it's for real!"

"Colonel, what do you mean for real?"

"They are going on a bombing mission off the coast of France."

"George," said the Major shaking her head, "they are not ready! They could all be killed!"

"Nothing I can do about it, Major. You have your orders. 10 minutes Margret!"

Major Hayes burst into the 10th barracks and began shouting orders. "Attention ladies. You have 10 minutes to put on your flight suits and collect your gear for a mission over France so move it now."

The women all froze staring at the Major like a deer caught in headlights not understanding the order. "What the hell are you standing around for!?" shrieked Major Hayes marching through the barracks and back, "get your flight suits on, put on your heavy jackets, don your mae west and don't forget your .45. I want to see you ready and your toes on this red line right now, move it, move it. You women are going to war so get your head out of your ass!"

The women scurried as quickly as they could and were ready in no time. Major Hayes stepped up then down the length of the barracks inspecting her girls. They were far from perfect but time was ticking away. "I don't know how we are going to win this war with such a rag-tag group of misfits. You had better shape-up and fast because the Colonel is waiting for you in the briefing room right now so straighten your ass up and MOVE OUT!" As Hayes watched her women scurry out of the barracks door she was fearful she may not see many of them alive again. Hayes wiped a tear from her cheek.

The crew of 'The Albatross' walked past their plane on the way to meet with Colonel Daniels. They saw the ladies of the ground crew feverishly slaving away fueling the plane and loading strange types of bombs in the bomb bay. "What kind of bombs are those, Marie?" The co-pilot, Lt. Kelli Blankenship, asked the plane's bombardier.

"I believe those are depth charges," said Marie.

"Depth charges? Those are used against submarines," noted Kelli.

"They're putting real ammo in our .30 cals," commented the waist gunner Lt. Julie Taylor, "This looks like the real thing."

The briefing room accommodated the 155 crew members and 12 alternates for 16 B-25 bombers the pilots of the 366 escorts. They all took a seat, the Captains and their crew sat together.

'The Albatross' crew consisted of Capt. Jennifer Edwards, co-pilot Lt. Kelli Blankenship, navigator Lt. Jetta Woodrell, bombardier Lt. Marie Trembley, the 2 waist gunners Lt. Terasa Gallos and Lt. Julie Taylor, top turret gunner Lt. Sandy O'Malley and tail gunner Lt. Joanna Owens. They all watched as Colonel Daniels explained the mission.

"Ladies, I am aware that you have limited bombing experience and no combat training," started Daniels. "But we have a vital mission that needs to be flown without delay. A group of 12 German subs have been sighted on the surface heading to their home port in Lorient, France. They are in no big hurry only moving at 12 knots which gives you plenty of time to head them off. A British Lancaster is tailing them so we know the subs position.

"The biggest problem you will encounter is that you are going to have to fly over a part of France that has many fighter air bases. You may go undetected but don't count on that. They will scramble fighters to intercept you.

"Commander Cyndy Bowie of the 366th and Captain Hannah Sherman will be escorting you to the target and back. Their 28 P-38s should keep the enemy fighter planes busy but keep your eyes open for bandits. Accompanying Commander Bowie's squadron will be a reconnaissance aircraft to film your bombing run.

"Your cruising speed is 300 miles an hour at 20,000 feet. You should meet the subs in a little more than an hour, then drop to 1500 feet and get into formation for your bomb run. You will be dropping depth charges. Your navigator and co-pilot will be trained on how to arm and set the depth on the bombs right after this briefing so I need you people to stay here. The subs' coordinates will be radioed to you an hour after you take off. Keep your speed steady, stay on your heading and you should not have any problem finding your target. Ladies remember your training, stay focused on your jobs…try not to be distracted."

A messenger interrupted Daniels with a note. "More bad news…the Lancaster ran out of fuel and crashed killing all six crew members. They radioed their final position before they hit the ocean. As long as the subs do not change course, you should still be able to find them. If you run short of fuel, drop your load and return to base. These subs already have a high price tag…don't make it any higher. That is all, good luck ladies."

"Dismissed," said Major Hayes. "Colonel you did not tell them that if they fail, they will be disbanded."

"They have enough to worry about, Major."

CHAPTER 17

THE BOMBING RUN

Captain Edwards gave a big smile and thumbs up out her pilot's window before roaring down the runway at top speed as the women of the ground crew cheered them on. The B-25s are much smaller then the larger B-17s and B-24s so four of the medium bombers can take off side by side at one time. In less than two minutes, all 16 B-25s were airborne and on course for their target. They immediately climbed to 20,000 feet. The crew donned their masks that provided oxygen and zipped up their shearing leather bomber's jackets because the temperatures at that altitude are well below zero.

P-38 Lightning

Once the 10th had taken off, Commander Bowie and her P-38s rumbled down the runway in the same fashion. They would not have any trouble catching the B-25s because the P-38s were faster. The P-38 was a single seated fighter bomber. It was a big plane nearly as long and as wide as a B-25. The 38's most notable characteristic was the twin booms behind the wings each housing a Allison V-1710, 1150 hp, turbo-charged engine propelling a 38 up to 414 mph.

Chatter on the intercom was light. Captain Edwards wanted the channel clear incase they spotted any incoming fighters. "Pilot from Navigator," said Jetta.

"Go ahead Lieutenant," replied Captain Edwards.

"We are entering French aerospace."

"Crew from Pilot, we are over France; keep sharp and watch out for enemy fighters."

"What other kind of fighters are there?" mumbled Teresa.

Again the intercom was quiet. "I guess the Germans don't want to come out and play this morning," said Kelli.

After nearly half an hour, Jetta called the pilot, "Pilot from Navigator."

"Go ahead Navigator."

"We are leaving French aerospace. Target should be visible in 10 minutes," Jetta was always very formal on the intercom.

"Navigator from Pilot, break radio silence and inform Commander Bowie of our position and inform her we are dropping to 1500 feet. Everyone watch for those subs.

The second they see us they will panic and try to submerge."

"'Black Widow' to 'Albatross'. I am the lead plane Captain…I will make these decisions," said Captain Jacqueline Natalia of the 'Black Widow'.

"As you wish, Captain…what are your orders?"

"Black Widow' to squadron, drop to 1500 feet."

"Pilot from Navigator."

"Go ahead Jetta."

"One minute to target."

The squadron arrived at the proposed point where the subs were supposed to be, but the sea was empty.

"C'mon you guys show yourselves," mumbled Captain Edwards, looking out her window.

"Anyone see the subs?" the Captain demanded on the intercom.

"Negative Captain, just a lot of open water," reported Joanna.

"Jetta, could you have made a mistake?" asked Jennifer.

"Give me a minute….no Captain, we are where we should be," reported Jetta.

"Oh crap," Jennifer muttered. "Keep looking ladies."

"'Black Widow' to squadron. They are not here. RTB, Return to base."

"This is 'The Albatross'. We have a job to do. We will make small circles and hopefully they will turn up. Try to stay together in a tight formation."

"This is 'Black Widow'. I'm ordering all planes to return to base now."

"Go if you want…'The Angry Albatross' is staying until we drop out of the sky."

"Captain, we can't stay here too long or our fuel will run out," said Kelli.

"Kelli you have a skill for stating the obvious."

All of the 25s stayed. After a while the flight had still not seen the subs. "Jetta, speak to me," said Captain Edwards breaking protocol after not sighting the subs for 20 minutes.

"I recalculated the numbers, time in the air, air speed; we are in the right place. The Germans may have changed course or altered their speed or submerged when the Lancaster crashed," reported Jetta.

"Damn," whispered Captain Edwards.

¥

Colonel Daniels sat at his desk nervously tapping a pencil on a stack of reports he was supposed to be reviewing before filing. He could not think of anything else but his girls.

"I'm here to have their quarters cleared out and made ready for a group of real men flyers," said General Jimmy Thomas poking his fat head into Daniels' office.

"Aren't you being premature, General?"

"They are overdue. I'm being practical. Women have no place in the Army, Colonel."

"Get out of my office, Thomas," ordered Daniels sternly.

Major Hayes was pacing anxiously across her office that adjoined Colonel Daniels'. She watched Thomas storm through and out the door. She gently rapped on the Colonel's door. "Come in Maggie," said Daniels. "I need a drink. How about you?"

"Yes, please," said Hayes in a whisper.

Then Master Sergeant Pam Morrison, the lead engineer on the base, came into Daniels' office, "I have those requisition forms you asked me for Colonel," she said putting more leaves of paper on Daniels' desk.

"Care for a belt, Sergeant? We are having one."

"Thank you, Colonel."

"Pam you would know best…they are late returning, aren't they? Should I be worried?"

"FUCK YES YOU SHOULD BE WORRIED!" exclaimed Pam loudly before she realized with whom she was addressing and then put her hand over her mouth. "Sorry," she said softly.

"What do you think might have happen…what's going on?" asked Daniels.

"Well," started Pam upon downing Daniels' drink then holding up her glass for another shot of his Scotch Whiskey. "Well, they could have stayed too long over the target and went into the drink. They could have encountered a mass of enemy fighters and went into the drink. Or they hit their target but got lost on the way home and again they went into the drink. Or best case…they will be limping in here any moment with dry fuel tanks."

"What are their chances Pam?"

"A bunch of girls flying an unskilled bombing mission over hostile territory half hour over due…I…have already packed my bags to go back to the states."

The trio glanced at each other before Daniels sat down at his desk slowly and hung his head low.

¥

"We can only stay a few more minutes." said Captain Natalia of the 'Black Widow'.

"I not leaving until I bomb submarines," demanded Jennifer.

"You will do as ordered Edwards or I will see you court marshaled."

"You do what you want, Natalia. I'm staying her to the last second."

"THAT IS IT! WE RETURN TO BASE NOW!" ordered Natalia.

"Go if you feel you must," insisted Jennifer, "I'm staying!"

"AND YOU ARE GOING INTO THE STOCKADE WHEN WE GET BACK TO BASE…."

"I SEE THEM, I SEE THEM. 11 NO 10 O'CLOCK NORTH WEST," shouted a tail gunner of another plane.

"Yup, there they are," reported Captain Edwards. "Bombardier from Pilot, align your bombing run, we don't have much time."

"'Black Widow' to 'Albatross'. Captain Edwards I'm not going to tell you again…"

"Captain we are to high for a bomb run," said Marie. "We need to drop to 500 feet."

"What are you saying, Marie?"

"We are too high to hit the subs. We need to be at 500 feet."

"'Albatross' to squadron…drop to 500 feet for bomb run."

"We can't bomb from 500," said Natalia.

The squadron dropped to 500 feet.

"BANDITS, BANDITS 1 O'CLOCK HIGH," came a voice on the intercom.

"Not a problem," reported Commander Bowie.

Commander Bowie and her 38s engaged the handful of Me-109s while the flight started their bombing run. Sailors popped out of two of the subs and manned their deck guns. They started taking pot shots at the 25s. "I'll take care of them," reported Commander Bowie. She and her wing woman Captain Alice Brokoski strafed the two subs silencing the guns."

"Damn Commander, save some fun for the rest of us," said Lt. Betsy Carson.

The other subs simultaneously began to crash dive. Marie noted how quickly the subs were submerging. Being an able mathematician, her brain quickly went into overdrive on its own calculating the length of the subs, estimated dive angle and time the planes needed to be in position. She came up with the necessary numbers without jotting anything down.

Marie left her position and climbed into the top turret bubble to see where the other planes were. "What the hell are you doing Marie?" complained Sandy, "I'm busy here."

Marie didn't answer but slid down to the Pilot. "Jennifer, order the rest of the flight to stay in a tight formation and drop their bombs exactly when I do in 30 seconds," said Marie.

"Marie!..." said Captain Edwards.

Marie stopped her decent into the bombardier's position to look at Jennifer with her dark brown eyes wide open. "Trust me Jennifer…20 seconds."

"This is 'The Albatross' to squadron. I'm switching you over to my bombardier Marie."

Marie's voice punched through Captain Natalia's complaining. "This is Lieutenant Marie Trembley of 'The Albatross'. Set the charges at 70 feet and drop when I do in 15 seconds. Ten…Five, four, threeee twoooo," said Marie looking through her bomb site, "aaaaaand one." Marie pressed the button releasing the payload. "BOMBS AWAY!" she shouted.

The rest of the squadron dropped their bombs just as Marie did. They ignored the orders from Captain Jacqueline Natalia not to listen to Marie. The crews of the 10th liked Jennifer much better than Natalia. "Anyone see anything?" asked Captain Edwards. "Any secondary explosions?"

"Only the splash when the bombs hit the water Capt.," Joanna reported from the tail.

"I can't be sure if we hit anything or not," said another tail gunner.

"We're going around again to see what happened," said Jennifer.

"No you are not, Captain Edwards," said Natalia. "You are going back to base to face a court martial."

"Well in that case, I guess we are going around again," said Captain Edwards.

"I got you covered Jennifer," said Commander Bowie. "Alice and I will watch for bandits."

"You all are in so much trouble," said Captain Natalia.

The rest of the squadron started on the two hour flight back to Hardwick. There was nothing more they could do anyhow. Captain Edwards dropped to 50 feet. By the time 'The Albatross' returned to the target, there was not much to see. The Atlantic was on fire, there was so much oil and debris in the ocean visibility was nil. "Start our cameras," ordered Captain Edwards.

Just then, a sub surfaced. When the hatch on the conning tower opened, a sailor climbed out but was engulfed by a stream of fire. The sudden in flux of air ignited the gasses inside the boat. It was nothing more than a coffin filled with smoke and flames. A smile came to Jennifer Edwards face when she realized the subs where destroyed. However, it was a sad smile when she realized they had just killed countless numbers of sailors. "Let's go home," she said.

CHAPTER 18

RETURN TO BASE TO FACE CHARGES

The ladies of the ground crews cheered the arrival of their particular aircraft as it touched down on the tarmac. A proud Colonel Daniels was in the tower at Hardwick counting the B-25s as they landed. 11, 12, 13, 14 and 15. Just 15, one was missing, 'The Angry Albatross', as well as the two 38s and the reconnaissance plane. Daniels and his aide scanned the horizon with binoculars searching for their loss aircraft but no sign of the planes. Daniels stayed in the tower for nearly an hour refusing to give up on his last airplane until it was time to start filling out paper work.

"THERE THEY ARE!!" shouted a tower controller. There was 'The Albatross' limping to base on one engine.

"Captain Edwards, what's wrong with your plane? Where you attacked by fighters? Do you need medical assistance?" Daniels frantically asked on the tower radio.

"No, not yet, Colonel. I'm out of gas and I'm coming in hot."

Daniels quickly punched the fire alarm signaling the fire trucks and ambulances to speed out to meet 'The Albatross'.

Jennifer lowered the landing gear. "Be ready to cut the engine Kelli, I'll hold her steady."

"Ahhhh Jennifer," responded Kelli, "the engine is cut…were out of gas."

"HANG ON!!" hollered Jennifer.

The plane slammed down on the runway with a thump dropping everyone into their seats or on the floor. Captain Edwards pumped the brakes so not to burn them out. The plane slowed to a stop at the very end of the runway.

"YEAH!" hollered the Captain out of breath before giving Kelli a big hug. As the crew slide out of the plane, they were met by the fire truck and several JEEPs carrying ground crew, friends and Colonel Daniels. Everyone was smiling and cheering.

"I'm glad you made it back, Captain Edwards," said Daniels with a smile,

"We're glad to be back, Colonel," replied Jennifer with a smile and salute. "Please develop our film from the fore and aft cameras of 'The Albatross'. I think you will find it satisfactory."

"Jennifer, walk with me," said Colonel Daniels. The two left the rest of the crew members. "Captain Natalia has filed insubordination charges against you. I'm sorry Jennifer; you are confined to quarters pending a hearing."

¥

Jennifer was a Captain so she had her own quarters. It was a single room, larger than most, with her bed, a closet, a dresser with a full length mirror on the wall next to the door and she had her own writing table with a desk. The sheet rock walls were painted white. She wondered what was going to happen to her. After a couple of hours, Major Hayes knocked on her door.

"Captain, Colonel Daniels wants you in his office right now."

"Thank you Major," said Jennifer struggling to her feet. She crossed the compound to Daniels office with Major Hayes two steps behind her.

Jennifer entered Daniels' office, came to attention, and snapped off a salute.

Daniels saluted back, "At ease Captain. That will be all Major." Major Hayes saluted before leaving the room.

"Sir, before you say anything, I did what I saw had to be done in the situation and I would have to face a court martial again because I would do it all over."

"Damn glad to hear it, Captain," said Daniels. "Jennifer, 'I was only following orders' has become a widely used poor excuse for the many blunders in this war. The reason we will win this conflict is because our American soldiers can think for themselves. We need those kind of people…You are that kind of person…Group Captain Edwards (similar to a Colonel)."

"Say what now?"

"I have debriefed the bombardiers and spoke with the Captains. I'm promoting you; you are the leader of the 10th."

"What about Natalia?"

"She's going home. I'm sure there are floors that need mopping or dictation to be taken in the states. Congratulations Jennifer. We are having a celebration party in the officers club. After all, it is not everyday we sink 12 of Herr Hitler's best boats. Are you coming?"

"Yes Sir!" said Jennifer with her smile.

CHAPTER 19

AVENGER FIELD

Virginia caught a hop, a military transport plane going in her direction, (usually a DC-3), from New Castle to Avenger Field in Sweetwater, Texas. During the six hour flight, she had a chance to see much of the country from the air because it was an absolutely gorgeous clear day and the plane flew at 1500 feet. The time in the air also gave the girl a chance to adjust to the idea of her new assignment. Virginia decided she enjoyed flying and looked forward to being up in the bombers but did not look forward to being shot at by Germans.

Avenger Field was the airbase base the WASPs used as their training camp. Colonel Daniels enrolled all the women he selected for his squadron in the WASP program to teach them how to fly the bombers the Army way. The woman in charge, Jackie Cochran, was none to happy with the idea but could say little about it because she did not wish to offend General Arnold. Colonel Daniels' periodic short term intruding trainees were allowed to join the group even though the American Bomber Girls did not meet WASP specifications. The American Bomber Girls were usually younger than the required age and much smaller.

Virginia was to join the class of WASPs already in session to learn how to navigate and operate the radio. She begrudgingly had to surrender her Sergeant stripes and citations on her uniform when she started working with the WASPs. Colonel Daniels explained that she had to be a WASP and not to forget that she was a part of a top secret mission.

Virginia had to bunk in the barracks with the other girls just like she did at Ft. Des Moines through out her basic training with the WACs. Unlike WAC training, she was exempt from doing calisthenics but had to spend more time studying navigation techniques and radio codes. Colonel Daniels wanted Virginia combat ready as soon as possible. Her absence from the athletic field did not go unnoticed, nor did the fact that Virginia did not meet the WASP height prerequisite of 5 foot 7 inches, nor was she 21 years old, the WASP minimum age requirement. The WASPs did not say anything to the new girl though she piqued their curiosity. They did speak about her special privileges amongst themselves.

The classes at Avenger Field were easy enough; however, Virginia did not like Sweetwater at all. It was hot and dry and the wind blew 30 bears continuously from sunup to sundown. It was a good thing she was mentally exhausted at the end of the day or she would never have been able to fall asleep at night.

The normal WASP training program was six months long. Virginia was there at Avenger for only a month. She was not a pilot so all that the girl had to concern herself with was navigation, radio codes and proper military paper work. Also map reading that she could do in her sleep so......nothing to worry about.

Virginia found navigation most interesting as well as cigarettes. Like the men, the WASPs were issued cool, healthy, filter free tobacco products. A WASP named Gloria, the only lady that Virginia befriended, taught

Virginia how to inhale the invigorating smoke without hacking her head off. She tried it for about a week before deciding that smoking was not for her and gave up the nasty habit. Virginia was a smart girl.

Virginia found navigation the most interesting part of her education. In addition to map reading, she learned about all the most modern instruments for keeping a bomber on course. All the devices in the world would be useless without Virginia's knowledge of math. Once she mastered the equipment, she climbed into an enclosed metal case shaped like an airplane with no windows. There Virginia learned how to navigate on instruments alone because she could not look out of the box. She spent many an hour in the simulator, not because she had to but because she thought it was fun.

Virginia also learned about 'Dead Reckoning'. She did not care much for the name of the navigation technique but did find it useful. 'Dead Reckoning' is the process of calculating the airplane's position by using its constant speed, direction and time in the air from a fixed starting point. It is extremely accurate. All she needed was a good map, a compass and a watch.

After her classroom and simulation training was done, Virginia had her first real hands-on training in an actual airplane. She donned a flight suit then climbed into the back seat of a Texan T-6 trainer. Her friend Gloria was the pilot who would be credited for the hours flown. Gloria, a 22 year old accomplished flyer who had already commanded a T-6 before, thought it a good idea to leave the canopy open so Virginia could enjoy the view. Virginia had never been in such a small open airplane before. Once airborne, she tried to crawl under her seat.

That flight was meant to be Virginia's opportunity to demonstrate her ability to apply all she learned about navigation. She had a problem with the altitude and the open cockpit. The girl found navigating difficult while lying on the floor with her eyes shut. To make matters worse, her instructors turned out to see the young girl navigate for the first time.

A half-hour passed before Virginia managed to poke her head up from under the seat and peek over the side of the plane toward the ground. She was feeling a bit more at ease when Gloria maintained level flight but when Gloria banked hard to starboard, Virginia was right back under her seat. Gloria was able to cover for her friend well by pretending to talk on the radio to Virginia giving proper radio codes supposedly from the navigator. It worked and everyone was pleased with Virginia's first time as a navigator.

The flights leading up to Virginia's graduation were flawless and beyond expectations. She did not only fly on the Texan but on the large bombers such as a B-17 and a B-25. Virginia marched with the graduation class, celebrated with the classmates afterwards and was on a morning hop for Hardwick, England before she could sober up.

CHAPTER 20

VIRGINIA GOES TO ENGLAND

Things moved quickly in Colonel Daniels' outfit. Upon landing at Hardwick, Major Hayes showed Virginia to her room that she would share with a lieutenant. After given about 30 minutes to get settled in the new surroundings, she was in Colonel Daniels' office.

Daniels bestowed the rank of lieutenant on Virginia and pinned the bars on her uniform himself. Also she received a citation which stated that Virginia was an USAAF Navigator and was entitled to all the rights and privileges that came with the rank. When she arrived at Hardwick, there were no openings for a navigator on the B-25s. Virginia's name was placed at the bottom of the duty roster.

While waiting for an assignment, she and the other alternates waiting for a spot to open up did what they could to help out with the ground crews. When she went on leave, Virginia hung with those same girls in downtown Cambridge…not the American Bomber Girls.

¥

After their immensely successful raid on the German U-boats, the American Bomber Girls earned their place at

Hardwick, or 'Hard Dick' as the girls called their base. They all chuckled to themselves each time someone said Hardwick… and cockpit...and cocktails. All the girls laughed save Marie. The French and Cree Canadian could not make the connection.

The American Bomber Girls finished their last weeks of training. The pilots learned how to power up or down the plane to get into or out of trouble. The gunners practiced on ground targets firing from a moving truck. Once they mastered shooting from a moving base, they went aloft in their plane to shoot towed targets at 15,000 feet.

All the members of the crews, whether pilot, gunner, or navigator, had to learn how to parachute out of a plane. In the event a B-25 was going down, the crew had a chance to jump from the plane. They were tethered to the exit so the parachute would open on its own. After training on the ground, the ladies had to make one jump. Once airborne, all the women leapt from a perfectly good airplane. All except Kelli who had to be pitched out of the door of a DC-3 screaming.

Hardwick was also the home of an RAF squadron. The British men did not have a problem sharing their base with the American girls. In fact they enjoyed the periodic welcomed distraction of seeing the good looking American lasses strolling the base in their flight suits, dark glasses and .45s.

Also sharing the base were the fly girls of the 366 fighter group. The unit was made of 32 P-38 fighters. The 366th was led by Commander Cyndy Bowie and Captain Hannah Sherman.

Cyndy Bowie, a 23 year old from upstate New York, was one of the original 1074 WASPs. After graduating top of her class, she was the first to boss a heavy. The American girl had an illustrious career with the WASPs highlighted by setting down a B-17 without a drop of fuel left in the gas tank. The maintenance crew failed to fill the plane's tanks…an act of sabotage frequently perpetrated on the WASPs by American men who were offended by women flying warplanes. Also the reason the WASPs had so many casualties.

Colonel Daniels picked Cyndy for his unit after she had to leave the WASPs due to a terminal liver disorder. The girl was chubbier than most of the American Bomber Girls so instead of being put on a B-25, she was given a P-38.

The 366th had just one job…protect the bombers of the 10th. With the addition of a 100 gallon external, self sealing fuel tank under the wing, the P-38s could stay with the bombers all the way to their target and back to Hardwick and shoot down German fighters.

The Air Force Base was commanded by a tall thin officer named General James 'Jimmy' Thomas who constantly had a stogie clenched in his teeth. Even though the base at Hardwick ran smoothly, he could always find something to complain about. In addition, he never stopped bitching about having the 'girls' on the base.

CHAPTER 21

THE MISSION OVER SAINT-NAZAIRE

With their training behind them, the American Bomber Girls were put on alert in January, 1943. Everyone knew that the time was short until they would be fly their first real bombing mission. After two days, Major Hayes rousted the women from their sleep before dawn. "Briefing in 30 minutes," she announced.

The crew of 'The Albatross' passed before their plane on the way to the huge operations hall for the briefing. They paused for a moment to watch the women of the ground crew fuel up the warbird and load it with 300 pounders. Inside the hall, the ladies took there seats along with the rest of the girls from the 10th as well as the fighter group the 366th. They talked amongst themselves about most everything until Colonel Daniels entered the room.

"Ten hut," said Major Hayes.

"At ease ladies, be seated," said Daniels.

Colonel Daniels opened the curtain at the front of the great hall exposing a map that was as large as the whole wall. It displayed South England and Northern France, Belgium and Northern Germany.

"Well ladies this is it, your first real bombing mission. After the shellacking you gave those German subs, I am confident you will do well," he lied. "Your target is the navel base and submarine pens at Saint-Nazaire on the coast of central France."

The British bombed the base earlier this morning so if it is still burning, you will have no trouble finding it. To curtail losses, you will fly around France instead of directly over German airbases. This will add another 50 miles to your trip but will reduce fighter contact. You will stay at 26,000 until you get to your target and then drop to 1500 feet for your bomb run. You will be on oxygen so keep your masks on. If you see surface ships, DO NOT ATTACK THEM. I hope I'm clear about that. Stay in formation.

"The P-38s from the 366th will be at 36,000 feet keeping you in sight the whole way to the target and back. If any enemy fighters scramble Commander Bowie will drop down to intercept and destroy them before they get you. As usual, there are a number of targets between here and Saint-Nazaire. We don't think the Germans will scramble fighters until you turn toward the coast. Bombardiers, don't try and hit the pens. They are much too strong and your bombs will have no effect. Just destroy the area outside the pens."

Are there any questions? Good. Dismissed," Colonel Daniels was never one to answer questions.

The American Bomber Girls all piled into their planes and did their final checklist before the pilots fired up the engines. Through the plane's open window, Jennifer gave a big smile and traditional thumbs up before throttling up the twin engine bomber and roaring down the runway with three other B-25s on her flanks. The women of the flight crews waved them on. They had done all they could do. The small planes were once again airborne in less than two minutes.

"Come starboard to 0101 degrees," said the navigator Lt. Jetta Woodrell to put the plane on course.

"Starboard 0101," responded Jennifer.

"We are taking a different route to the same location we were at on our last mission," said Kelli.

"Yeah that's true," said Jennifer. "Colonel Daniels doesn't want us to encounter fighters."

"I bet Cyndy would rather take the shorter route and meet up with fighters before adding all the extra time and miles."

"I bet you would too, Kelli. You know we should get a flat in Cambridge tonight and really get plowed."

"Sounds good to me," said Kelli.

The girls found that talking as if the mission was over and seeing themselves back at base eased the tension.

There was little chatter on the intercom during the flight. There was no communication with base or other planes. Strict radio silence was enforced. "Hey Teresa," said Joanna.

"What?" she replied.

"Aren't you Catholic? How do you feel about bombing Germans on a Sunday?"

"Nothing I can do about it, Joanna."

"Please keep the chatter to a minimum," said Jennifer.

"In a minute, Captain. Teresa, I heard the Pope absolve the Jews for sinking the 'Titanic'," said Joanna.

"You're so dumb, Joanna, the 'Titanic' was sunk by an iceberg," said Teresa.

"Iceberg, Steinberg, Weinberg, they are all Jewish," said Joanna. Indeed once in a while the girls would tell a joke over the wire. The girls could be heard quietly chuckling.

"Pilot from Navigator. Come port to heading 095," said Jetta.

"Port 095," repeated Jennifer. "Ladies lets keep the channel clear."

"One more story, Captain," said Sandy.

"Saaaandy, I said no."

"So this guy goes downtown to pick up a hooker," said Sandy ignoring her Captain.

"What town?" asked Joanna.

"The town your mother lives in so shut the fuck up Joanna I'm telling a story," replied Sandy. The whole crew laughed including Jennifer. "So this guy picks up a 10 dollar whore and she gives him crabs."

"Yup, sounds like my mother," said Joanna.

"Anyhow he sees the hooker two nights later and complains about getting the crabs. The whore says…hee

hee…what do you expect for 10 dollars…shrimp scampi?"

Once again the whole crew busted put in laughter.

"Alright fun time is over…call out those fighters when you see them," said Jennifer.

"Why didn't anyone tell me about fun time?" said Joanna.

"Jennifer we are heading south along the coast of France. You can bet the Krauts know we are here. They may scramble fighters soon," said Jetta.

"Right Jetta. This is the Captain to crew. Watch for fighters and call them out when you see them."

No sooner had Jennifer made her announcement than the top turret gunner Sandy O'Malley saw Messerschmitts. "Bandits, bandits 2 o'clock high." She pulled back the bolt on her 50 cal. and nervously waited for the Germans to attack.

The Fighters stayed high up out of machine gun range. They did not dive or fire on the flight.

"What are they doing?" Sandy thought aloud.

"We have to wait and see," said Jennifer. Jennifer broke radio silence, "Fox leader to all Foxes. Don't fire on the Messerschmitts until fired upon. Jetta, get me Cyndy."

"Fox leader from Commander Bowie," came the response from Jetta's hail.

"Cyndy, do you see those German fighters?" asked Jennifer.

"Yes, but not for long."

"Let's leave them alone for now, Cyndy. Don't give away your position."

"What?? You don't want us to attack the fighters? Jennifer have you gone nuts?"

The German fighters flew off.

"They are probably just checking out our numbers. They will be back," said Jennifer.

After being in the air a short time longer, tail gunner Lt. Joanna Owens reported bandits. "Bandits on our tail…and there are a bunch of them."

Jennifer immediately radioed Cyndy to attack. Commander Bowie was more than happy to drop down 10,000 feet and chop up the German fighters just as they began their attack run on the B-25s. The Germans found themselves more concern with staying alive than firing on the bombers.

Cyndy scored a hit vaporizing a Me-109. Her wing girl, Alice, also shot one down. She watched as the pilot managed to bail out of the plane and parachute to the ground.

The guns of 'The Albatross' commenced firing on the fighters. "A pint of ale for anyone who gets a fighter," said Jennifer.

"Look at that, you owe Sandy one…correction two already Captain," said port waist gunner Teresa Gallo.

"You owe me one too," insisted starboard gunner Julie Taylor.

"I'm gonna go broke," said Jennifer.

"I got one," said Joanna, "Hey the krauts are leaving."

"Pilot from Navigator, target in 10 minutes."

After a few minutes, the Germans regrouped and attacked the B-25s again. They did not fare any better that time and flew off. A few of the P-38 pursued them but were immediately called back by a very irate Commander Bowie. Everyone could hear Cyndy give her pilots three shades of hell. It was good for a laugh. Commander Bowie told her pilots to stay with the flight of B-25s. The Germans continued their hit and run tactics all the way to the target.

As the group of 36 American bombers approached Saint-Nazaire, the anti-aircraft batteries cut lose. There were quite a few guns despite being pounded by the British just a few hours earlier. The German spotters were accurate and a B-25 suffered a direct hit in the fuel tank in the port wing. The women on 'The Albatross' watched the bomber split in two before spiraling toward earth with the entire crew on board. A second B-25 was hit and was on fire. Six of the crew bailed out. A third American war bird took a shell to the port engine but the pilot set her plane down safely.

"Pilot from Navigator. Target in two Minutes," said Jetta.

"Bombardier from Pilot, Marie, you have the plane."

Marie balled up her long jet black hair and stuffed it under her lieutenant cap. She watched through the eye piece of the bomb site waiting for the marine base at Saint-Nazaire to appear. Marie kept the plane level. That was when the warplane was most vulnerable because it could not take any evasive actions to avoid flak bursts or enemy fighters. Despite the anti-aircraft flak, the fighters attacked again. The P-38s kept the Me-109s at bay but not without losing two of their own and an additional B-25 who lost both engines, five girls leapt from the plane dropping nose first toward Earth.

Finally Marie had a clear view of the town below. She pressed the button with her thumb releasing the bombs from the bay below the plane. "Bombs away," she quietly said into the intercom.

"Fox leader to all Foxes," said Jennifer, "mission accomplished, return to base." The fighters followed the planes back over the Atlantic.

¥

The American Bomber Girls' squadron was well shot-up when they began to land at Harwick. Some of the planes came in with only one wheel. The pilot sat the medium bomber screeching across the runway before skidding into the grass spinning in circles. Other planes had no landing gear and simply ditched into the grass along the tarmac. Most of the planes carried wounded who had to be carefully stretchered to an ambulance. Most of the planes carried dead crew members. Some had to be removed from the war bird by Sergeant Pam Morrison's women with axes. It was always a disturbing sight that few ever got accustomed to.

The women had lost five B-25s and three P-38. Unlike the mission to sink the subs, the American Bomber Girls lost friends in the raid on Saint-Nazaire. Cheerful, joking, smiling faces at the breakfast table were gone not to ever come back. Just like the men's squadron, the women had to deal with their loss. Though they tried not to, some of the women began to sob in front of Colonel Daniels at the debriefing. (Debriefing was where the Colonel and his staff spoke with the flyers one-on-one about the mission). Many of the women were successful in being behind the barracks before beginning to cry. Seeing their dead crew mates being chopped out of a crashed aircraft was hard to understand or comprehend.

Colonel Daniels was a career soldier who saw his friends get blown apart in WW I. The men in his unit cooped with it. He was not prepared to deal with emotional women. He did not foresee that and had no contingency plan. He tried to explain that in war, people die…he was just plain useless. Not all the American Bomber Girls broke down. The majority of them wanted to get back in the air and avenge their friend's death.

Fortunately, there was a unit of British nurses from the Auxiliary Territorial Service (ATS) on the base. The women of the ATS were involved in the war longer than the Americans and had seen these emotional breakdowns in the men so they were experienced with talking about friends dying, with the American girls. The British women were very good at calming the distraught Americans. They consoled the women individually or in groups. Because of the ATS, the women were able to get into their airplanes.

After the debriefing at Hardwick, the women were given a 24 hour pass as usual. The girls inflicted a tremendous amount of damage to the sub pens but the USAAF sent a fleet of B-17s to Saint-Nazaire and permanently put the pens out of action by fire bombing the base.

CHAPTER 22

THE BRIEFING

At the onset of WW II, the Germans could not conceive a time that the populace would ever have to scramble for an air raid shelter. Not one bomb, artillery shell, or even a bullet landed on the Father Land during WW 1 so in August of 1940, the Germans were stupefied to see a squadron of British bombers over Berlin. Sure the civilians all had wine kellers to crawl into but those were not sufficient to protect the people in the big cities.

Hock Bunker, Hamburg

To solve that problem, the Germans built bomb-proof buildings called 'Hoch Bunkers' which were high above ground bomb shelters. The hoch bunker was quicker and cheaper to build than the underground bunkers because there was no excavating involved. The buildings were 20 to 60 feet high with six to nine feet thick concrete walls reinforced with rebar. Some of the hoch bunkers were sloped at the bottom to deflect a bomb and were most effective. A hoch bunker could protect up to 500 people from allied bombings. According to well kept records by the Germans, there were only five people ever killed in a hoch bunker and that was after a direct hit by an allied bomb.

Following the war, in an effort to purge the country of everything NAZI, the allies attempted to destroy the bunkers. After their best efforts all the allies could do was put a crack in the wall of a hoch bunker so most are still standing today. Some are in ruins while others have been transformed into museums, offices, schools and hospitals.

Anti-aircraft guns (19)

In a major contradiction, the hoch bunker was constructed to protect the German population; however, the Deutchers put four large anti-aircraft cannons on the top of a bunker making them a target of the USAAF. Hamburg had two such bunkers and in July of 1943, Hamburg became a major target. 'Operation Gomorrah' commenced with the objective of destroying Hamburg's submarine factories, submarine ports (pens) and oil refineries. The British Lancasters bombed at night while the American heavies pounded Hamburg by day. First, the American Bomber Girls were sent in to clear out the anti-aircraft guns.

¥

The women knew a mission was coming up because they were on alert. They had sometime to prepare themselves for another go around with German fighters and flak. Finally, Captain Edwards woke the crews of the 10th for an early morning briefing. As the crew of 'The Albatross' walked past their war bird, Marie noted some less than subtle changes to the plane.

"Hey, where's my bubble on the front of the plane?" she announced, "There is a metal cone over my spot. How the hell am I supposed to see out of that?" The bombardier quickly approached the engineer on duty. "What's going on?" she demanded.

"Talk to the Colonel, Marie…he's changing things up some," explained Pam Morrison, the unit's engineer.

Marie just shook her head, threw her arms in the air, and joined the rest of the crew already taking their seats at the briefing hall. Everyone settled down when Colonel Daniels stood up in front of the group of 320 women. He opened the curtain at the front of the hall that exposed a map of England, Northern France and Northern Germany.

"Ladies," started Colonel Daniels, "You will be spear heading 'Operation Gomorrah'. For the next week the USAAF will be pounding Hamburg, Germany. Your job today is to weaken their defenses such as their anti-aircraft batteries.

"Your planes are being modified. You will not be carrying any bombs. Instead, the front of your B-25 will be outfitted with four 50 caliber machine guns and a large 75mm M4 field cannon. These big guns are the same ones used in field artillery and on tanks, they pack a real wallop. The bombardier will be responsible for reloading these cannons. The co-pilot will fly the plane while the pilot aims and fires the new guns and the cannon. The pilot has two buttons on the steering column. One will fire the 50 cals while the other fires the cannon…don't get them mixed up!

"You bombardiers don't read anything into this. You are doing a hell of a great job but we need something different on this mission. Your training on loading the big gun will follow this briefing."

75mm canon w/ 4 Browning 50 cals w/ belt feeds (20)

The room that once was filled with voices before the meeting begun were suddenly silent as the Colonel continued, "The plan is for your squadron to fly at 50 feet over the North Sea from Hard Dick...I mean Hardwick!" There was some laughter in the room. "Sorry ladies I know some of you have chosen that for the base nick name...Anyhow, it should take you two hours to reach the Elbe River where you will turn south toward Hamburg," explained Daniels as he pointed to the great map on the large wall.

"Your main objective is to seek out and destroy the anti-aircraft guns on the top of two large towers. When you find them, use your cannon to blast them out of existence. They shouldn't be too hard to find seeing how they will be firing on you as soon as you reach the edge of town.

"After you take out the anti-aircraft batteries feel free to shoot up any other target you find. Do not waste your energy on the big buildings the batteries are sitting on...you won't do any good.

"Commander Cyndy Bowie and Hannah Sherman's P-38 will provide cover to and from the target. In addition, Captain Tony Anderson and his squadron of B-24 bombers will be on a decoy bombing mission to Bremerhaven. There are several targets along your route to Hamburg...Amsterdam, Bremen, Norderstedt and Bremerhaven. The Germans won't scramble their fighters until they have an idea what target we are after. That is if they see you at all. Any questions?"

Yes there were a thousand questions but they would be answered as the day progressed. Marie and the other bombardiers attended their class on how to load the tank gun. Jennifer and the other pilots were shown the triggers on the steering column.

It was after lunch before the 10th was on the flight line revving the powerful engines of the B-25s. The tower gave the signal to take off, a green flare, and Captain Edwards lifted her foot from the brake pedal sending the small bomber careening down the runway flanked by three other war birds. Right away the squadron was in flight just feet above the waves of the North Sea cruising at 300 mile per hour.

"This is the part I hate," said Kelli.

"What's that?" responded Jennifer.

"Two hours of sitting and waiting with nothing much to do but watch for fighters. We should put a bar on this plane."

"Are you nervous?"

"No, I'm excited…but not nervous."

"Well I can't have my co-pilot be so bored, maybe I can spice up the trip a bit. This is Fox leader to all Foxes….let's test out that new cannon. Just aim and fire at will."

Marie had already loaded the big gun and put a magazine of shells in the 50 cal. "Already when you are Captain," she said.

Jennifer pushed the button and fired the tank gun. The blast was outside the aircraft as the shell dislodged from the gun. The recoil of the cannon rattled the plane so bad that the crew believed it was going to break a part.

"Wow," said Jennifer, "I'm glad we did that now instead of over the target."

After being in the air for more than an hour, the American Bomber girls tried something new and different. Each medium Mitchell bomber released a cloud of shredded tin foil from the back of their air plane. The tin foil was called 'chaff' and was very successful at creating a false blip on the enemy RADAR. In addition, the Germans continued to receive contradicting reports from their forward spotters so they had no idea where the American bombers were. They scrambled a squadron of fighters in hopes that they might find the American Bomber Girls.

After two uneventful hours, the flight made their turn down the Elbe River that flowed through Hamburg. The city came into view and Jennifer marveled at how beautiful the old town was...but not for very much longer. "Fox leader to all Foxes. They have not seen us. Let's make the first pass at those subs in the pens. Use our new cannon and the 50 cals. Stay in formation and follow me in," ordered Captain Edwards.

The flight of 36 planes broke up into six waves with six planes in each wave. The American Bomber Girls attacked, flying into town with their 50 caliber machine guns blaring supported by their 75 mm staying in perfect formation. They hit several subs being resupplied before their voyage to sea. The women also demolished some submarines in dry dock. There were rows of torpedoes ready to be loaded on to the U-boats that lit up like the 4th of July.

Suddenly the anti-aircraft guns let loose accompanied by diving Me-109's. "Cyndy, We have company!!" said Jennifer.

"We're coming," said Cyndy.

Cyndy kept the German fighters distracted while Jennifer and her squadron made some evasive maneuvers to elude the guns. "Fox leader, we have to take out those guns...follow me in."

Jennifer charged the flak towers. She fired two snappy shots from the 75 mm at the enemy cannons before pulling up over the big guns. "Did you hit anything?" asked another pilot.

"No, only impacted into the side of the tower." reported Jennifer.

The pilot of the next B-25 attacked the hoch bunker. She dropped down low just above the roof tops over an avenue leading to the tower. Not low enough, her plane was hit repeatedly by the enemy's guns. The starboard engine and gas tank were hit…they burst into flames and the B-25 dug a trench as it crashed into the houses in the city below. The next B-25 made her attack run…she was quickly hit by the skilled German gunners and she spun out of control crashing into the streets of Hamburg killing all 8 American Bomber Girls onboard.

The next B-25 swooped in behind the previous. "Lukka, veer off you have no cover," ordered Jennifer.

"I'm going in," announced the captain.

It was 19 year old Lukka Brown, the youngest and the most inexperienced of the squadron, who was piloting 'The Maiden of the Skies'. She flew exceptionally low between Hamburg's hundred year old houses, eluding the anti-aircraft batteries. However three unmolested fighters closed in behind the lone American gun ship. She knew the fighters were on her tail so she increased her speed making gradual evasive actions. Lukka knew she had only one slight chance to hit the German's guns at high speed. The 109s unloaded on her plane.

"Pilot from Waist gunner, we loss the tail gunner," announced the waist gunner.

"Pilot from Navigator, Lukka, our top turret gunner has been hit."

"Pilot to crew, we stay in formation…keep the fighters busy."

"Navigator from Waist gunner…the starboard waist gunner has been hit…do something!!!"

"I'm on my way," said the plane's Navigator.

"There are too many fighters Lukka…we need to veer off," said her co-pilot.

Lukka held her plane steady staying on target even though the German fighter's attack was relentless. The shells of the Messerschmitts continued to rip and shred the small American bomber.

Suddenly, the lead German fighter behind Lukka's plane turned to vapor forcing the two other 109's to spin out of control smashing into the houses below. "The fighters have crashed, Lukka…Blast them bastards," said Hannah with her P-38.

Lukka took her foot off the gas and slowed her war bird to near stall speed before launching a shell into the top of the flak tower followed by two others. The big guns blew, followed by several explosions as ordnance on the tower ignited followed by a chain reaction of ordnances exploding leaving the top of the hoch bunker ablaze. The flames from the burning tower lick the bottom of the 'The Maiden of the Skies' as she flew over the tower.

"Anybody want cheese on that Hamburg?" asked Jennifer.

"No, but can I get fries with that?" said Lukka.

CHAPTER 23

HEADING HOME

Hamburg was on fire. The B-25's pounded the central city while firing on the anti-aircraft guns. With the flak tower taken out and the German fighters engaged with the American P-38s, the American Bomber Girls could roam the skies virtually unmolested. They broke formation and flew in pairs in search of good targets. Without a bomb load, the B-25s could fly like fighters.

Captain Lukka's plane was well shot up so she had to return to base but not without a pair of 38s watching over her all the way back to Hardwick. Jennifer and Kelli followed the rail road tracks out of town and sure enough they found a train running away town. The American Bomber Girls opened their attack with the blaring 50 caliber machine guns that were mounted in the nose of the plane. Each of the six inch long shells easily tore through the box cars until one of them obliterated. Once the big gun was locked and loaded, Jennifer let loose a shell into a railroad car. The freight car blew into a thousand pieces derailing the train behind it. Pilots always found exploding gasoline very rewarding.

Once 'The Albatross' reached the locomotive, Jennifer drove home a 75 mm shell down its smoke stack. The engine burst into flames sending shards of metal in all directions. After the locomotive blew the rest of the freight cars derailed and piled up on the other some exploding into flames.

Of all the dumb luck, another train was coming into town. The engineer must not have received word that Hamburg was ablaze. Jennifer let the train pass below 'The Albatross' before strafing the box cars with her 50 cals. She then circled back around and annihilated the locomotive with two 75 mm shells. The train derailed sending rail cars stacking on top of one another like a toy train set.

♫I've been working on the raiiiiilroad all the live long day, ♫ sang Kelli.

♫I've been working on the raiiilroad just to pass the time away, ♫ Jennifer and Kelli sang together laughing.

The other American Bomber Girls found worthy targets also. Some tore up the airport nesting 50 caliber slugs into the control tower. The shells passed through the glass windows before bouncing around the control room five or six times tearing up equipment. The American Bomber Girls then parked a 75 mm shell in the tower just for good measure. In addition, there was no shortage of German aircraft neatly arranged in rows. Most were civilian planes but what the hell they explode just like war birds.

50 cal bullet

The American Bomber Girls created further havoc. A squadron of four B-25s attacked the submarine factory while in a perfect formation. The Germans had several nearly completed U-Boats in dry dock. On the first pass by the B-25s sprayed the subs with their menacing 50 calibers. The shells pierced the hulls of the boats and then like before ricocheted inside the subs. The American bombers stayed in a tight formation as they came around for a second pass hammering the factory with a relentless barrage of 75 mm shells supported by the 50 cals.

"Lead Fox to all Foxes," came Jennifer's voice over the intercom, "Time to head home ladies." She ordered the group to form ranks north of town over the Elbe.

The American Bomber Girls took their place in formation leaving the burning burg behind. The mission was a tremendous success but they were not leaving unscathed, four planes crashed before the flak towers were destroyed. Thirty two dead comrades were left behind.

¥

Back at Hardwick, Virginia sat alone in the grass on the side of the landing strip with her legs crossed watching and waiting for the squadron to return. She often wondered if she was ever going to have a chance to go on a mission. She wondered how well she would do on a mission. *'Just get the plane to the target and back,'* she thought to herself. *'How hard could that be?'*

Like everyone else, when the flight became visible on the horizon, she got to her feet and joined the ground crew ready to help out. "Sixteen, seventeen, eighteen," like everyone else she quietly counted the returning small bombers as they touched down and the fire alarm sounded. Once again many were damaged hobbling onto the runway with one engine or ditching into the grass without landing gear.

The ground crews, each woman responsible for the maintenance of just one particular plane, were also diligent watching waiting for their plane to appear. They were exuberant when their plane landed…and teared up when it did not come back. Like always, Virginia assisted in removing the wounded and the dead from the planes. Like the men's squadron, the women suffered casualties. 'The Angry Albatross' always came back from a mission without a scratch which was strange because Jennifer flew the lead plane which was usually machine gun fodder for the fighters.

The mission was followed by a debriefing. Following the debriefing, the crews would watch the movies filmed by the war bird's onboard cameras. Like the men, the women would all cheer when an enemy plane was obliterated or a building was blown up.

After the mission, Colonel Daniels gave everyone a 24 hour pass. It was time to get cleaned up, slip into a dress uniform and make ready for a good time in Cambridge. Downtown Cambridge was only a short car or JEEP ride away from Hardwick. The women had a favorite pub to hang out in. It served cold beer which is unusual for England and the best Irish stout ale in the world.

The crew of 'The Albatross' always sat together. "You all had a good mission today," said Virginia while passing their table.

"Excuse you!" said Jennifer, "Are you talking to us!!?"

"You must be lost little girl," said Kelli, "How old are you anyway? 10? Why don't you go back to your friends. This table is for real flyers."

"Silly plebe," said Sandy, before they all laughed at Virginia together.

Virginia swallowed hard. "Sure Lieutenant. What was I thinking?" Virginia could hear them laughing as she walked away. "Whores!" she said aloud. Being that she had not yet flown a mission, she was not considered suitable company for the crew of 'The Albatross'.

Virginia was 16 years old in a pub in England. Since she was dressed in a American lieutenant uniform, she could drink any damn thing she wanted. She never had to pay for her drinks because the girl was by far the cutest in the joint and there was always a social service man ready to buy her a beer. Virginia's favorite drink was the Irish ale. It was a strong drink, not customarily ordered by a woman let alone a small girl. She hung with the maintenance crews, the other men from the base and some of the locals. They were all impressed by Virginia's ability to slam Irish Ales and still win at darts.

Of course Virginia, like all the other American Bomber Girls, was hit on by the men. She was 16 but since she was a Bomber Girl and a Lieutenant in the USAAF, she had to be at least 18 or 19 years old and available. The idea of a 16 year old being a navigator on a B-25 was a hard to believe. Virginia always went back to the base alone.

"I'm turning in," said Kelli.

"What do ya mean Kelli, it's early?" protested Jennifer.

"I'm really tired and I'm not feeling right. I had a great time but I think I want to go back to base and to bed."

"Ok, suit yourself. I'll see you at breakfast."

"Sure, good night everyone." said the co-pilot of 'The Angry Albatross'. She returned to the base by herself while the others closed the pub before catching a ride home.

¥

Late the following morning there was a knock on Captain Edward's door. She opened it to find Marie nervously fidgeting.

"Captain, Kelli is AWOL," said Marie.

"What?" demanded Jennifer.

"Absent without leave."

"I know what AWOL means…"

"She did not return from town last night. Colonel Daniels wants to see you right away." instructed Marie.

"I'm on my way," said Jennifer.

"Kelli returned to the base early, Colonel. Way before the rest of us," said Jennifer.

"She did not sleep in her bunk last night," said Daniels.

"Something is not right," said Jennifer. "She said that she was heading home."

"Jennifer, could she have met someone outside the bar?" asked the Colonel.

"No Colonel, Kelli would not go anywhere else and not tell me. Colonel Daniels, request permission to go and look for her."

"Denied, everyone is confided to base. Jennifer THAT is an order."

After a while, Colonel Daniels was informed that Kelli was found in a bombed-out building not far from the pub. Jennifer was camped out in the Colonel's office and heard the call come in. She was eager to go to town with him. "Maybe you should stay here Captain," said Daniels.

"Kelli is one of my girls, and my friend," said Jennifer.

"It's not a good idea."

"Just try and stop me…Ah Sir!"

"Alright, come along."

When the two left Daniels' office, they were met by the rest of the crew of 'The Albatross'. "What are you doing?" demanded Daniels.

"Going with you, we want to see Kelli," they all responded.

Daniels looked them over, "Ok get into the truck," he said.

CHAPTER 24

THEY FOUND KELLI

The women did not say much while they were being bounced around in the back of a truck with bad suspension. Nor did they complain about how chilly the morning air was or how the wind blew through the truck's closed flaps. It was not a very merry ride into town. Sandy, as always, was first to break the silence. "I hope she is not hurt. Or not to badly injured. I like Kelli. What do you know Captain?"

"I don't know anything, Sandy. I know she wasn't feeling good. Maybe she stopped to rest and fell asleep. We will all know soon enough."

The ride to Cambridge was not long. When the truck turned down the street where Kelli was found, there were many MPs about and a few men in regular street clothes. In addition, there was an ambulance with some American medics standing about. When the truck stopped, the ladies quickly filed out the back. Led by Colonel Daniels, none of them were ready for what they found in the building.

Kelli was there…standing upright…supported by her outstretched arms with ropes tied to her wrists and then the ropes were secured to the bare burnt beams above her head. The American girl's head hug low on her lifeless body. The Co-pilot was still wearing her neatly pressed uniform pants and regulation shoes; however, her jacket and shirt laid in tatters around her feet. Kelli had several deep and bloody cuts across her bare chest and abdomen made by a sharp knife. There was a major stab wound in her lower back that finally ended the girl's life.

"Everyone out," ordered Jennifer.

"Captain we want to stay and…," said Sandy.

"GET OUT!!" shouted the Captain. "What happened here Colonel?" asked Jennifer.

"As far as the investigators can tell, German spies captured her as she made her way back to base. They tortured Kelli for information," said Daniels.

"What kind of information?" questioned Jennifer. "Did Kelli know something the rest of us don't?"

"I can't imagine what they thought Kelli knew that they didn't already know. They must have thought she knew something important to risk being exposed. I hope it wasn't about your mission…"

"What? What's that….."

"Nothing Captain, I was just thinking aloud," said Daniels before walking away.

Jennifer joined Daniels again. "Why do the MPs leave her hanging there naked? Why don't they cut her down?" she asked.

"The investigators need time to gather all the evidence they can. We best go outside."

Out on the sidewalk, the rest of the girls were sobbing and consoling one another. "Colonel, we need a bombing mission…now!" demanded Jennifer.

"You got it, Jenn."

¥

The service for Kelli was held in the American Cemetery on the edge of Hardwick. The service was attended by a much larger than normal crowd because Kelli was very popular. Some commented oh how they would miss Kelli's cheerful disposition and personality, warped sense of humor and bright smile.

The next day, a uniformed man arrived at Kelli's parent's house in Springfield, Illinois. He carried a small wooden box with a Distinguished Service Cross (the highest medal presented save the Congressional Medal of Honor) which he presented to the American Bomber Girl's confused parents. The officer also presented them with a letter signed by President Roosevelt expressing his condolences for their loss and explained that Kelli died in the service of her country. The man said that their daughter received a full military service in a place that will be disclosed to them sometime later.

¥

Jennifer wanted and needed a mission. After two days, the squadron was put on alert. A day later, Colonel Daniels called a briefing for a mission. As always, the normally talkative voices in the briefing hall went silent when Daniels stepped to the front of the room. He announced that that day's target was going to be Schweinfurt, then those in the room moaned in unison.

Ball bearings and oil are what keeps an army on the move. One is no good without the other. The Germans were receiving plenty of oil from Romania in exchange for their help keeping the Soviets in check at the Romanian/ Russian frontier. The ball bearings came from Schweinfurt, Germany. The USAAF lost many B-17s on bombing runs to Schweinfurt because the town was heavily fortified with anti-aircraft batteries and a few squadrons of fighters.

Colonel Daniels explained that the British hit the bearing plant the night before. A squadron of 120 B-17s had already been sent to bomb the city that day.

"This is where you ladies can use your special talents. You will carry less fuel than normal and since your crew weighs much less than the men, you will carry larger bombs. You are going to fly over France at 26,000 feet. Stay south of Frankfurt and navigate towards the desirable target of Wurzburg. At the last minute, the navigator of the lead plane will make a one degree adjustment to Schweinfurt. We hope this will catch the Krauts protecting the wrong city. Just follow Captain Edwards when she makes her course correction. A decoy squadron of empty B-24s will be sent across the coast of North Germany to confuse the German's fighter command and maybe score a bunch of Me-109's in the process. Good luck ladies…Dismissed."

"Why are you so quiet Captain?" asked Sandy as they walked to 'The Albatross'. "I never knew you to be at a loss for words."

Jennifer stopped and addressed what was left of her crew. "We are flying for the first time without Kelli…I miss her already. Jetta Woodrell has gone on sick leave too. We will have two new crew members today. One new member would be alright but two new girls who have never seen combat? That can't be good!! We are the lead plane! Everyone is counting on us to perform well or our mission will fail. You girls keep an eye on the new women. If they lose their nerve or panic, you just let me know right away."

"You got it Captain," they all agreed.

When the crew arrived at the plane, they meet the new members. The first was a smiling bubbly woman. "Lieutenant Anastasia Blake reporting for duty, Capt. You can call me Honey. I'm your new co-pilot. And Capt., my condolences for the loss of Kelli. I knew her and I hope to fill her job well."

"Thank you Lieutenant."

The new navigator was a small young girl who looked like she just stepped out of kindergarten. "I'm Lieutenant Virginia White, Navigator, Captain Edwards," said Virginia sheepishly trying not to make eye contact.

"You!! Why you!!? Have you ever been on a plane before? You're too young to be a good navigator. How old are you? 12?"

"I get that alot, Captain. I'll get us to the target and back," insisted Virginia.

"This is not going to happen. I need a replacement for my replacement."

The crew could hear the other B- 25s revving up. "Captain, there isn't time," said Marie, "We have to be on the flight line NOW!"

Jennifer hesitated for a moment to think things through. "Alright. You girls could not have picked a worst mission to start out on. Just try to keep your cool when things get hot. Remember your training, you got it?"

"Yes Captain," the girls replied. As the woman climbed into "The Albatross', Jennifer grabbed Virginia by her bomber's jacket. "Don't even think about screwing up, Plebe!" she growled at the much smaller girl.

"OK! Captain," replied Virginia, angrily before climbing into the plane.

Jennifer so wanted to replace Virginia. *'Not a good way to start a mission'* she thought to herself.

After the check list, Jennifer fired up 'The Angry Albatross' and in no time at all the squadron was airborne.

¥

The first mission over Schweinfurt was the worst bombing mission for all concerned. The town was well protected by a multitude of ack-ack (anti-aircraft) batteries and fighter bases. The squadrons of American B-17s and British Lancers suffered unacceptable losses.

"Lieutenant White, check on the starboard waist gunner. I think she's been hit!" ordered Jennifer who kinked her neck to the right so to speak with Virginia seated behind the co-pilot.

"Right Captain," replied Virginia stepping away from the maps and charts sprawled across her Navigator's table. She hesitated for a moment looking out her window to see a B-25 on fire, spiraling toward Earth.

Virginia had to tend to the injured starboard waist gunner so she quickly tip toed her way on the thin catwalk through the bomb bay and between the racks that held the bomber's cargo of 300 pound bombs. She then slid through a short tunnel to the waist gunners. Virginia sat on the floor of the cramped space next to Julie the gunner. Julie had caught a piece of shrapnel from a bullet fired by the Fw-190. The hot metal passed through the plane's thin aluminum external skin before slicing through Julie's side. She was parked on her butt with her back against the plane's bulkhead and her bloody hands pressed against the wound quietly moaning.

"You're going to be alright," said Virginia, not really knowing how badly the gunner was cut. It was just something people say in situations such as that one. Fortunately, the hot shrapnel cauterized the veins and the capillaries in the wound so Virginia was able to staunch the bleeding with a simple gauze pressure bandage. "What are you doing!!?" she demanded of the gunner who was struggling to her feet. "You are hurt and need to lay flat until we get back to base."

"Nothin' doin'. Help me back to my feet. I got work that needs to be done," said Julie.

"Julie, be sensible. If you start bleeding again, I may not be able to stop it. Stay down."

"That's what you New York Yankees do, but us Florida girls live to fight."

"I'm an Indians fan from Ohio."

"Just help me to my gun, Gini."

Virginia chose not to argue and assisted the thin 5' 4" 19 year old to her 30 caliber machine gun. She was done tending to Julie so once again she slipped back through the bomb bay and found the way back to her post behind the co-pilot's seat.

Virginia quickly did the math calculating their position. "Pilot from Navigator, target in two minutes," she reported over the intercom.

"Bombardier from Pilot, you have the plane."

Lt. Marie Trembley's small five foot frame was crouched down in the Plexiglas bubble in the front of the aircraft. Hunched over the bomb site, she watched as the target came into view. She was in control of the plane calculating air speed and wind direction. The Germans tried to mask her view of the target with a smoke screen but it was too little too late. "40 seconds to target," she reported before Marie shook her head tossing her long black hair out of her face and then looking through the eye piece of the bomb site.

After what seemed to be an eternity of continually being bounced around by exploding flak, Marie reported 20 seconds. When the girl was sure the plane was properly positioned, her thumb pressed the button that released the plane's deadly payload. "Bombs away!!" she shouted into her intercom.

The American Bomber Girls lost eight of their B-25's on their first mission to Schweinfurt. Of the 28 planes that returned, three were shot up so bad that they were beyond repair. In addition, 26 dead women, including Lieutenant Julie Taylor from the 'Albatross', were removed from the planes. The 10th had to stand down (not fly any missions) until new planes and new crews could be assigned to their squadron.

CHAPTER 25

COLONEL DANIELS EXPLAINS THEIR TRUE AND UNUSUAL MISSION

It was an unscheduled surprise briefing called by the American Bomber Girls' commanding officer Colonel George Daniels. Those attending the meeting were the bomber crews of the Flying 10th as well as the fighter pilots of the 366th. These squadrons were not on alert nor were there any missions planned. In fact, the American Bomber Girls were ordered to stand down until further notice.

The women were in a reasonably good mood after their successful bombing of Schweinfurt. That was one factory that was never used again. So the girls gathered in the large briefing hall chatting amongst themselves as usual until Colonel Daniels step into the room.

"Ten Hut," said Major Hayes. Everyone in the hall came to attention.

"At ease and be seated ladies," said Daniels. He hesitated for a moment looking at all the curious eyes staring back at him. "Ladies," he started, "It is time to inform you of your true mission here in Europe."

"Ten Hut," Major Hayes said again as General Thomas, the base Commander, entered the hall from the back and rapidly walked down the isle to the front of the room. The squadron came to attention.

"He's the reason our base is called Hard Dick," Jennifer whispered to Honey who tried not to laugh but could not help herself. "Shhhhh, you'll get us put in the stockade," said Jennifer.

"At ease," said Thomas. "Colonel Daniels I would like to address the squadron."

"Sure General, they're all yours," said Daniels. *'Oh boy. Now what?'* he thought to himself.

"Ladies, I have made it no secret that I DO NOT like seeing you women flying war planes. It is NOT ladylike. Nor is it ladylike for women to kill people."

"We are not ladies, General," a girl shouted from the back and causing the others to laugh.

"In addition," continued Thomas, ignoring the interruption, "I have NOT made it a secret that you are NOT welcome on my air base." He stopped and eyed the quiet crowd. "I just wanted to congratulate you on a job well done at Schweinfurt.

"You are doing a great job and are a credit to the American fighting spirit. You have my condolences for your losses…but when you fight like soldiers…you will die like soldiers. You have my thanks and blessing. Continue on." Thomas was done and exited the room the same direction he came in.

"Wow, Ole Hard Dick is full of surprises," whispered Honey.

After Thomas left the room, Colonel Daniels started over. "Ladies," he said, "It is time to inform you of your true mission here in Europe. What I'm about to tell you is top, top secret so listen up. Just as Thomas said, you have performed well and met all the high standards and expectations of the United States Army Air Corp. Now is the time to tell you your real mission."

Daniels hesitated for a really long moment. "Where do I start? I thought this would be much easier. I'll come straight to the facts. Many of the American Bomber Girls have already been captured by the Germans and we know that the German soldiers have been taking liberties with our girls. We were certain this would happen.

"You all know why you have been selected for this unit. You may not speak of the reasons but you all have one thing in common. All the pilots and co-pilots lost their license in civilian life. Many of you were WACs, WAVs or even WASPs before you were given an honorable discharge…you all know why you were drummed out of military service.

"I have recruited you for that same reason. We need you for a special kind of warfare…a type of warfare that the enemy will not be able to fight. Many of you will be captured by the Germans that is a cold hard fact." The Colonel suddenly looked older and paused as he spoke. "What the High Command wants you to do…or wants you to be…well ordered me to ask you…is for you girls to be a living biological weapon of mass destruction."

A rumbling rose up from those in attendance in the room much like a dormant volcano awaking after a millennium-long nap. "What I tell you here today is top secret. I can not stress that enough. If you are caught telling anyone about what we discuss here, anyone at all, you WILL be shot as a traitor," continued the Colonel. "The plan is to inject each of you with a mutated man-made virus. The bug will not harm you in any way…that we know about. If you are captured and taken advantage of, the one who attacks you will die a horrible miserable agonizing death in three to four months."

Once again the volcano rumbled to life.
"Ah…Colonel," interrupted a young waist gunner, "I never finished the sixth grade, I don't understand a word you are saying. Can you repeat that in plain American?"

"Ok here it is…you each will get a shot in the arm that WILL infect you with a sexually transmitted killer virus. The bug will reduce the afflicted person's ability to fend off simple illnesses such as the common cold, so the sick person will die. The disease will not harm you but anyone who has sex with you, by force or otherwise, will get the disease and die in three to four months. Before they display symptoms of the bug, we hope they transfer the virus to someone else through sexual contact, who gives it to someone else, and so on.

"The disease has no symptoms at first and when found, it has no cure. The sick person will die. It will not affect you girls in any way. You will be carriers, an extremely deadly walking weapon. Much more dangerous than the men."

¥

The rumbling volcano exploded! "ARE YOU FUCKING KIDDING ME?"
"YOU'RE NUTS!"
"THIS IS SICK!"
"YOU HAVE GONE TOO FAR!"
"BEING MORE DANGEROUS THEN THE MEN…IS THAT SUPPOSED TO MAKE THIS IDEA IS LESS CRAZY?"
"HAS THE ARMY LOST IT'S FUCKING MIND?"

"I'M JOINING THE GERMAN ARMY!!"

Came the responses from the crowd of angry and hostile women.

"ATTENTION!" shouted Major Hayes, "COME TO ATTENTION!" she persisted but to no avail. The room was in an uproar and Colonel Daniels let the women get their complaints aired as they eventually quieted down on their own.

"Colonel, will we ever be cured from the bug? Or carry it around forever?" asked a girl.

"How long is forever for you, Tami?" replied Daniels.

Tami thought about it. "Never mind, Colonel," she said.

Once again the volcano came alive exploding into 400 voices speaking all at once.

"One more thing ladies," said Daniels trying to be heard over the rumbling and chaos. "One more thing," he repeated himself as the roar subsided. "Take the night to think this over. If you want to go to Cambridge then do so. Since Lieutenant Blankenship's death, we ask that you stay in groups of three or more and carry your .45 under your jacket. Don't be afraid to shoot first.

"You have until morning to decide if you wish to be a part of this operation… or not. If you chose not to, you will be replaced by someone who will. You'll be given an honorable discharge and sent home where you can live out your life. No one will think any less of what you have done here…you are already heroes."

The rumbling continued when Daniels dismissed the women and quickly left the briefing hall.

¥

MP presence was heavier than usual that night Jennifer and the crew from 'The Albatross' went to town together. They went to their favorite pub…and the last place they saw Kelli. The women all were seated at a round table away from the other patrons. They did not want to be heard so for the first time the women checked the place for hidden microphones. They didn't find any.

Before finding their seat, Jennifer took Virginia aside by the arm. "Virginia you did good up there," said Jennifer. "No one will call you a plebe anymore…not after Schweinfurt. Would you…I mean will you…stay on and be my navigator?'

"Sure Captain," said Virginia. Then the Pilot and the Navigator joined the others.

Jennifer gathered her crew together to discuss Colonel Daniels' crazy assed scheme. Before beginning, she ordered nine ales. There were only seven women but Jennifer ordered nine ales. The English waitress was quick to bring them their order. Two of the ales were set in front of two empty chairs.

"Why the extra beers?" asked Virginia.

"One is for Kelli and now the second is for Julie," explained Jennifer.

The waitress then brought out a sort of bunt cake made of pudding. Jennifer, being the leader tasted the cake first. "This is pretty good," she said while chewing, "what's it called?"

"Spotted Dick," announced the waitress. "I thought you would like it."

"Spotted what…" asked Jennifer.

"Dick!" said the waitress proudly.

Jennifer quietly gagged when she swallowed. "It's very good," she said. The girls were breathing hard trying desperately not to laugh watching their group Captain eat dick…that would be rude. "Here ya go everyone. Have some," ordered Jennifer spooning out some dick to the other American girls.

"Enjoy your dick ladies," said the waitress while going back to the kitchen.

Spotted Dick is British Pudding. It is made of suet pastry mixed with dried fruit, usually currants and/or raisins, rolled into a circular bunt cake. Suet, of course, is raw hard fat from animal loins and kidneys (I could not possibly make this up). In 2009, the name was changed to Spotted Richard. Who names their son Dick anyhow?

So the women were taking small bites of dick. "Have you ever had Dick like that, Gini?" Honey asked, hoping to entrap the young navigator.

"No I haven't," she said being her usual innocent self. "Do you like Dick Honey?" Boy, did not backfire on the older women.

"Yes I do…but I have never had dick like this," said Honey, "Have you Gini?" Some of the girls quietly chuckled.

"Leave her alone, Honey. Everyone just eat your dick so we don't insult our hostess," said Jennifer.

"This is the first time we've ever had a dick at this table," said Joanna. "Or the whole unit."

"Ok, I can't help it anymore…I have to laugh," said Teresa.

Talk was small while the women ate their Dick. Jennifer was first to bring up the subject at hand…she was a true leader. "This is an informal meeting so feel free to say what's on your mind off the record. We need to decide what to do about Colonel Daniels' plan."

"Gaaage," Teresa quietly coughed.

"So, I want to know what you all think," added Jennifer.

"Aaaaaack ahem ahem….," continued Teresa.

"Is something wrong, Lieutenant?" demanded Jennifer annoyed with the interruption.

"Sorry, I have a dick caught in my throat," said Teresa chuckling between gages.

"Eat another bite," said Joanna, "I swear you do this all the time. Your gullet must be the size of a pea."

Teresa had another bite and was fine. "May we continue, Sergeant?" asked Jennifer.

"Captain, I'm a Lieutenant," protested Teresa.

"Not for long."

Teresa sort of blushed with embarrassment. "Please continue Captain…I'll be quiet and chew my dick."

Like all tail gunners who cram themselves into the small space at the back of the B-25, Joanna was petit. She was 22 years old, short, weighed only 95 pounds and had dark hair and eyes. Joanna grew up alone on the mean streets of Newark, New Jersey. Her schooling was limited but she knew fire arms and had carried a loaded gun since she was nine years old. Daniels recruited Joanna from a federal prison where she was doing a life sentence for murder. If she came out of the war alive…she was promised a pardon. Joanna and Teresa, a pudgy young 19 year old of Italian decent, became fast friends, mostly because they were both from New Jersey.

"You girls are avoiding talking about this," said Jennifer.

"It sounds loony to me," said Marie. "The whole idea of using us…our bodies…as booby traps. It's nuts. I'm not at all sure I want to be a part of it."

"You want to go home?" asked Teresa who was just released from the hospital before the briefing.

"No I do not Teresa!" said Marie sternly. "I want to serve my country bombing Germans not by putting my ankles behind my ears!" Teresa quietly laughed. "Do you find something funny, Teresa?"

"No Marie," said Teresa, "nothin' funny at all."

"Ok let's calm down…we are just talking here," said Joanna quietly taking another bite of dick.

"I don't want to go home either," said Sandy.

"I don't think any of us want to quit," said Teresa.

"What is the Colonel not telling us?" asked Marie. "Why did the pilots lose their license? Did you lose yours Captain?"

"Yes, I did. It was the worst day of my life. You don't know why we were picked for this squadron Marie?"

"Should I?"

All the other girls knew why…why didn't Marie? "Because we are all dying from some sort of terminal disease," said Jennifer emphatically. "I have this thing in my head that will eventually cause my brain to shut down."

"Alright I'll talk about it too. I have a liver disorder," said Honey, "the doctors gave me 12 to 18 months to live. I probably won't live to see how this war turns out so hell yes I'll take the shot and keep flying."

The ladies were quietly passing glances back and forth. "The cat is definitely out of the bag now," said Jennifer. "When the Colonel offered me this position with 10th, I jumped all over it."

Sandy looked around, "We all did," she said. "So that's it, High Command hired us because none of us have anything to lose...that is so offensive."

"Insulting or not it is the truth," said Jennifer.

Silence once again fell over the group only to be broken by the barmaid who brought them all a round of Scotch Whiskey bought for them by an old Englishman. Being perfect guests in the old man's country, the girls raised their shot glass to salute the man before downing the shot in one gulp.

"So what do we do now?" said Joanna.

"Order another round of that whiskey, that was some good stuff," said Honey.

"You know what I mean. What are we going to tell the Colonel in the morning?" Joanna restated.

"I don't think 'we' have anything to do with it," said Marie, "Each of us can only decide for ourselves. We have 'til morning to decide."

"While you are deciding," continued Sandy, "think on this...some of us have never experienced sex and after taking the shot never will!"

The silence! This time it was deafening.

"You know I won't speak for anyone else but myself," said Virginia, who had remained quiet listening to the other's concerns up until now. "But I have been through way to much SHIT the past year just to give up and go back to stinkin' Ohio. I'd sooner face a battalion of angry Germans armed only with a pen knife before going back to Canton.

"Like the rest of you, I was destroyed when the doctor told me I was dying, but it has already been said and I agree that dying in a fiery B-25 spiraling toward Earth still beats the hell out of dying in bed screaming in pain.

"You know for this operation to work, we all would have to be sexed. You older girls may have been intimate in the past but I never have and have no plans to be sexed anytime soon. Dying without doin' it never crossed my mind until now...thanks Sandy." The girls all chuckled. "We never speak of what would happen to us if we get captured but it is no mystery. We are women and the German soldiers are men. What do you think they will do? Bake us a cake? Take us out to dinner? Write us some poetry? They will bang us like a snare drum and there will be not thing-one we can do to stop them." Virginia stopped for a moment and looked at the other girls hanging on her words. "I heard that sometimes even the men get raped by the Germans.

"If it is a question of taking the shot and keep flying or being sent home...I have no qualms about taking the shot."

"Out of the mouths of babes. Our youngest crew member is the brightest," said Jennifer.

"One question," said Marie, "what are qualms?'

"Virginia says she is taking the shot," said Honey. She drew a heavy sigh, "I have to keep on flying. I'm taking the shot."

"Yeah, I'm in," they all agreed save Marie.

"What? Aren't you gonna take the shot Marie? You will miss out on all the fun," said Jennifer.

Marie sighed too. "I can't let my country down...God save the Queen...I'll take the shot."

CHAPTER

26

THE MISSIONS

The young American girl remained with 'The Albatross'. After taking the shot, that made them all carriers of a dangerous killing virus, the American Bomber Girls continued their missions. After clobbering Schweinfurt, the women flew a combination of bombing runs and gunship attacks. At the end of August of '43, there was the bombing of Watten on the north coast of France on the Franco-Belgium border, just a short hop from Hardwick. The Germans were constructing a gigantic bomb-proof concrete bunker to house V-2 rockets.

V-2 Rocket poised for launch (21)

The V-2 was a multi-stage guided missile capable of delivering a warhead to London from France. It was the world's first Inter-Continental Ballistic Missile (ICBM). The concrete bunker at Watten was proposed to house 100 V-2 rockets, a liquid oxygen (rocket fuel) factory and a bomb-proof train station to bring in supplies for the missiles.

The bunker was never completed. The American Bomber Girls were a part of 'Operation Crossbow', a joint British and American plan to continue bombing the bunker while it was under construction. In addition, The Germans' grandiose idea of 100 V-2 rockets was way too ambitious. They lacked the means and materials for such an undertaking.

In September, the girls were a part of the on-going bombing of Mainz, Germany. In 1942 and again in 1944, the industrial city of Mainz located in Central Germany, was one of the USAAF's many cities slated for destruction. There were few (if any) missions to Mainz in 1943 so in September the American High Command opted to send the American Bomber Girls over the city. The American Generals had the idea that the Germans would be caught completely off guard by a surprise attack. The problem with the plan was that the Germans were ready for any assault on Mainz. They put up many fighters to intercept the American Bomber Girls.

Once again Jennifer fired up the engines of 'The Angry Albatross'. "Clear chucks," she shouted to the girls of the ground crew through her open pilot's window. The Group Captain smiled and then revved up the twin engines and rolled down the runway. The small squadron was once again airborne destined for Mainz.

The flight to their objective was only 650 miles and would take just over two hours. Colonel Daniels kept the ladies on short missions ever under the air cover of Cyndy Bowie and her 38s. The flight flew at 28,000 feet over the Franco-Belgium border before turning east at Bastogne then over Luxembourg. The route was longer than a direct flight but the American Bomber Girls avoided the many fighter bases in the Ruhr Valley. There were no targets of interest along their way and fewer fighter bases.

The summer of 1943 was absolutely beautiful. Not a cloud in the sky, hot and with little rain. Normally the weather turns cold and cloudy the last weeks of August but in '43 the temperature remained warm clear into mid October. Virginia did not experience any problems navigating the flight over France. The towns appeared below her right where they were supposed to be at just the right time according to her map and watch. She could clearly see the small French towns from her window through the cloudless azure sky. "Navigator to pilot, come port to 045," Virginia told Jennifer when it was time to turn toward the target.

"Pilot to crew, we are over Germany, watch for fighters."

"Bandits two o'clock," reported Joanna, "and there are a bunch of them."

The Focke-Wulf Fw 190s attacked at full throttle not giving an angry Commander Bowie a chance to dive down and defend the armada. The Germans immediately attacked a B-25 causing her to lose one engine. The crippled plane gingerly glided toward the ground. Two Fw 190s closed in on the damaged ship but Cyndy and Alice blew them out of the sky at point blank range. The injured B-25 turned towards base with a P-38 ensuring her safety on the trek back.

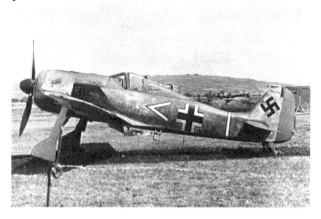

Focke-Wolfe Fw 190 (22)

The Focke-Wulf Fw 190 was a little single-seat fighter only 47 feet long with a slim 36 foot wing span. Its 1700 Horse power BMW 801 Dg propelled the plane at 440 MPH. The small plane carried two 13 MM MG 131 machine guns above the engine, two 20 mm MG 151 cannons in the wing roots and a 30 Mk 108 machine cannon firing through the propeller hub.

The fighters broke off their attack hoping to draw the American fighters from the war birds. That was not going to happen as Commander Bowie and her girls stayed with the squadron. The Germans saw that the American fighters were not going to give chase and quickly came around on what looked like a suicide mission. They successfully knocked down two B-25s but suffered heavy losses at the guns of the bombers and the American P-38s.

"Pilot from Navigator, target in 10 minutes."

"Bandits, bandits, 11 o'clock high," announced Sandy while swinging her turret around. She had become very good with her 50 caliber making only short bursts. Attacking fighters can bob and weave but just like any plane the Me-109 must fly straight to obtain a lock on its target. Sandy knew that and patiently waited for the few seconds the enemy fighter was most vulnerable before she fired her 50 cal blazing the German fighter and pilot. She knocked down two of the attacking German planes and forced the other two to veer off. "Like shooting pigs in a barrel," the turret gunner always said.

Jennifer kept control of the plane longer than usual due to all the fighters. "Pilot from Navigator, target in one minute."

"Pilot to bombardier, she's all yours. I hope I didn't screw you up."

"Not a chance Captain." Marie had no trouble finding the railroad station in her site. "Bombs away," she reported.

CHAPTER 27

LUITENANT MEGAN JACKSON

Lt. Megan Jackson woke to find herself pinned in her seat. She was the tail gunner on-board the 'Maid of Honor' that was riddled by fighter fire after leaving Mainz. Megan was unable to bail out after the Captain gave the order because a shell from a Fw-190 passed through the plane's outer skin and smashed into her right foot then ricocheted up into her shin destroying the tibia. Surprisingly, the injury did not hurt until the short, thin, 86 pound 20-year-old American Bomber Girl tried to slide out of her cramped space, then the pain shot up what was left of her right leg, through her hip and into the lower torso. Megan loudly moaned before settling back down into the padded seat.

"Heeeeeey," the Lieutenant shouted through the rest of the plane behind her with a southern draw. "Y'all there? I could use some help here! HEY!" There was no answer. Once again Megan attempted to free herself but her efforts were futile. Once again the pain shot across her hips and once again the girl slumped into the seat. "Damn," she cursed.

The German summer was hot and the sun began to beat down on the Plexiglas bubble that normally protected the tail gunner from the elements. Megan began to feel like an ant under a magnifying glass under that dome. She had to get out of the plane or the afternoon sun would fry her like that ant. Without water, she would not last long.

Fortunately, she did not have long to wait before a lone German soldier poked his helmeted head into the waist gunner's open window. The plane was quiet and appeared empty so he stepped through the waist gunner's window onto the scattered, empty, spent 30 caliber shell cartridges that covered the floor of the 'Maid of Honor'. He stumbled briefly on the dead port gunner lying face down on the floor. The German turned the flyer over and gasped in surprise to see it was a woman.

"Hey Fritz," said Megan calmly, "How about a little help here."

The soldier was shocked to hear a girl's voice on the plane and pointed his rifle at Megan. She immediately tossed her .45 onto the floor of the plane. It was useless to her. The military issued .45s were poorly built and hard to fire accurately unlike the Colt .45s. "Hilf mir," said Megan who learned some Deutsche from her grandmother when she was a child. "My ah, ah, ah, bein is hurt."

The German seemed to understand. He put down his gun and removed his helmet before coming to Megan's aid. The big blue eyed brawny uniformed man slide along side of Megan. He looked down on the petit American girl and could see that her pants leg was a torn, bloody mess.

The tail gunner's position is cramped enough for one but with two of them back there it was really snug. The German squeezed himself up against the plane's bulkhead just enough to run his arms under and about Megan's legs and back. He gazed into her sea blue eyes before lifting her up while still bent over at the waist. He tried not to, but could not help banging her foot against the side of the plane causing the woman to yelp and groan as he carried the American girl out of the plane and laid her on a cool grassy field. A few bumps while being pulled from the wreckage of the plane was still better than dying from heat stroke in the seat.

Megan tried to sit up and struggled to take off her shearing bomber's jacket because she was still warm. The German helped her with the coat by supporting her back. After she removed her jacket, Megan undid her top three buttons on her shirt then laid back down on her back.

"Wasser," Megan asked politely. The German again supported her while surrendering his canteen. She was thirsty and sucked down the better portion of his water supply.

Megan was from South Carolina. Her mother's family came from Bavaria three generations before the war. Her grandmother never learned English though she lived her entire life in the US. Her father's family was pit bull ownin', hog huntin' southern boys distantly related to Thomas 'Stonewall' Jackson, the Confederate General. Megan joined the WAVs to prove that she was a loyal American but was to be sent home when the Navy found out she was allergic to her own perspiration, a condition already acute and would soon kill her. She never thought she would be bombing her own people.

"Where is Switzerland?" asked Megan. The German did not understand. "Wo liegt die Schweitz?"

The German said something and pointed south.

"Danka shun. I'll be on my way now. Bye…I mean truss (c-ya)." Megan tried to stand but fell down on the grass and rolled onto her back moaning. "I reckon I ain't goin' nowhere," she said.

The German nervously chuckled at the girl then scooped her up and effortlessly carried her into a strand of tall chestnut trees before setting her down again. "What are you doing?" demanded Megan as if she didn't know.

The American girl did not protest when the soldier unbuttoned her shirt and undid her belt. He had no trouble peeling the girl out of her uniform because the clothes she wore were always to large for her small frame. He used his knife to remove her last stitch of clothing. Megan gasped but laid naked with her arms crossed against her chest staring off into the trees. She knew what was coming next but opted to do the task for which she was chosen. The German unbuttoned his pants and aped up on top of the American girl. She hardly made a sound…just a periodic quiet moan and yelp.

After the man finished doing his thing, he stood up and adjusted his uniform. Unbeknownst to him, another soldier was watching him rape Megan. He was standing at the edge of the chestnut tree forest where the 'Maid of Honor' rested. The two soldiers spoke for a moment. The second German wanted to have his way with the girl. He slowly walked over to Megan lying on the leaves staring off into the trees with the sun shining through the branches. The soldier nudged her in the ribs with the side of his foot. She folded her arms across her bare chest and kept them there while the German soldier did what they do to naked wounded defenseless American girls.

The second soldier was followed by two more Germans who found their way to the downed plane. When they were done, Megan turned her head to see the group of Germans talking amongst themselves. She could tell they were speaking about her because they kept throwing glances in her direction.

Megan laid still stretched out on the forest floor. She grinned for a moment knowing that those rapist where doomed to die shortly. No matter how healthy they were, the virus they now carried will kill them in three to four months. The wound on her right leg throbbed but it was not too terribly awful. She closed her eyes and rested wondering what was to become of her. Probably be taken to a POW camp somewhere. She laid under the chestnut tree listening to the birds constantly singing and the wind rustling the leaves on the huge trees. She felt the sun's warmth every now and then shine on her skin much like a summer's day at home. Megan didn't see the German soldier hovering over her, nor did the American Bomber Girl feel the two slugs fired into her chest from the soldier's luger.

The Germans did not want to get into trouble for raping an American prisoner. They buried Megan with her uniform in a shallow unmarked grave between the roots of the chestnut trees before returning to the plane just as a Major arrived. They explained that all the crew was dead or missing.

Once Megan was classified 'Missing in Action', an officer arrived at Megan's parents house from a letter from President Roosevelt with condolences for their daughter's death. Also the uniformed man presented the parents with a Distinguished Service Cross for Megan's sacrifice.

¥

Lt. Megan Jackson was found in 1948 by a team of American veterans who investigated crash sites in an effort to find the missing in action. She was returned to her home in South Carolina where her parents gave the Daughter of the Confederacy a proper military funeral.

Due to the well maintained records kept by the Germans, the men responsible for the American girl's death were tracked down. All had died on or about the same date due to an undisclosed illness. Two had wives who also died quickly thereafter leaving seven young children orphaned. The plan set in motion by the American Bomber Girls was coming to fruition.

The death toll from Megan being raped and then senselessly murdered was staggering. The figure was made higher by the Germans themselves. In 1940, the German High Command noted that the cost of their soldiers contracting a venereal disease was huge. The soldier had to take time from the war and there was also the expenditure of medicines to treat the virus which could have been used to save lives in the front.

So to rectify the problem, the German military sponsored safe brothels for their soldiers (sometimes the truth is unbelievable). Girls between the ages of 15 to 25 were rounded up in conquered cities such as Warsaw, Poland and Smolensk, Russia. If a woman older than say 30 was mistakenly kidnapped…she was shot. These kidnapped young healthy girls were put to work in the state run brothels. The men who came to the whore houses had to pay three marks and were given 15 minutes with the girls. A girl was expected to service 23 men a day (Really, this is all true).

Chances are good that one of the two single men who raped Megan took advantage of the brothels giving the American-made virus to the poor unfortunate sex slave who in turn gave the virus to maybe 20 men a day. That would be 140 men a week who spread the disease across the country before he himself succumbed to it. Even today's super computers can not count the cost to the German people in deaths and medical expenses attempting to save lives. All from one murdered American girl. Multiply that by 10 raped American flyers and the death toll is astronomical.

CHAPTER 28

THE MISSIONS

In October, 1943 the USAAF had to return to Schweinfurt.

"Schweinfurt?" said Jennifer in the briefing prior to the mission, "I thought we permanently put that plant out of business."

"The Germans have rebuilt what was left of the ball-bearing plant with slave labor," explained Colonel Daniels.

'Schweinfurt was the worst mission we were ever on,' Jennifer thought to herself, *'That is were we lost Julie.'*

Jennifer was concerned about the mission. Not for only her safety, that too, but for the safety of her crew and her squadron. The last time they flew to Schweinfurt she lost a crew member and three others were wounded. That was the only time anyone was hurt on her plane on any of her missions.

The American Bomber Girls did their job well on the mission to Schweinfurt. As before, the RAF lit up the town the night before so the target was easy to find…they just followed the smoke. The flight of B-25s flew east paralleling the coast of northern France before turning south and then east over Belgium. The women learned much more about flying since their last visit to Schweinfurt making the second trip much easier on the crew. The gunners on 'The Albatross' had time to practice their trade and were much better a knocking German fighters out of the sky.

Messerschmitt 110 (23)

The Germans sent a squadron of Messerschmitt 110s to intercept the American Bomber Girls. An Me-110 was a large, twin prop, well armed but poorly defended, unimpressive heavy fighter bomber that did not fly much faster than a B-25. It was 39 feet long with a wing span of 53 feet the same size as a P-38. The plane packed two 20mm cannons and four 7.92 mm fixed machine guns in the nose. It also had one 7.92 manually operated machine gun in the rear for defense. The Me-110 enjoyed success in the early days of the war until it encountered the American fighters or a well armed bomber. Then they were really just machine gun fodder for the sharp shooters on the Mitchells. Colonel Daniels once commented that the women were much better gunners than the men…though he had no paperwork to back up his claim.

In addition, the flight of B-25s always had Commander Cyndy Bowie and her P-38 air women ever close by protecting the bombers from German fighters.

The American Bomber Girls had 'Acceptable' losses. Only one (or sometimes two) B-25s and one or two P-38 per mission. There was always a constant supply of new planes and crews to replace those that were lost.

In November, of 1943, the American Bomber Girls returned to Mainz followed by a bombing mission on the industrialized Ruhr Valley. In December, the American Bomber Girls teamed up with the RAF squadron with whom they shared Hardwick. The British planned to force Germany to surrender by destroying Berlin, the capital of Germany from the air. The operation was called 'The Battle of Berlin'.

The British amassed 800 long-range bombers with an additional 18 Mosquito fighter bombers. The American Bomber Girls' squadron of 36 B-25s slipped into the center of the huge air armada and was well hidden with the Mosquitoes. When the flight was near the Ruhr Valley, the American B-25s, and the British Mosquitoes with their P-38 escorts, peeled away from the main group and surprised Essen. Their mission was to bomb the Krupp Manufacturing Plant. Krupp made parts for tanks, submarines, anti-aircraft guns, battleships and just about any other weapon. The allies made frequent raids on the factory but Krupp rebuilt with the use of slave labor. When the Americans arrived at Essen, there was no air raid siren, no anti-aircraft fire and no fighters scrambled. The B-25s and Mosquitoes had little to no trouble bombing their targets. The girls returned to base with no casualties.

¥

A nine year old German girl was home alone playing in her bedroom of her flat on the third floor of a apartment building in Essen. Her mother spent ten to twelve hours a day, six days a week, working at the Krupp factory churning out small motors for torpedoes. The mother had been bombed many times but always had sufficient warning and managed to scramble to the shelters below the factory unlike the slave labor who always suffered casualties. The girl's father was at the front…somewhere.

An elderly lady who lived next door, looking after her grandchildren during the day, checked in on the girl from time to time. The German girl did not understand the issues and problems of the world; all she understood was that she missed her mommy.

So one sunny beautiful morning the girl was in her bedroom playing with her toys and just being a good girl when she heard the rumble of a fleet of war birds over her city. There was no air raid siren and there was no firing of the anti-aircraft guns on the edge of town. From her window, she could see the squadron of small airplanes then she could see the belly of the planes open and then she could see the bombs begin to fall.

The girl was trapped. No time to run to the keller. All she could do was take a handful of blankets, a pillow and then slide under the bed and listen to the bombardment exploding in the city streets.

It is not easy to describe the sound of a falling bomb. It is much like the word 'hurl' with out the 'h' and a very long 'u'. Something like 'uuuuuuurl'. Then there is the ensuing explosion that sounds like 'boooooom'. The boom resonates for about 10 to 15 seconds overlapping other explosions. It is very loud and very terrifying.

There was a blast just outside of the girls building. The windows of her bedroom shattered scattering shards of broken glass on the floor. She reached up on her bed to grab her stuffed bear. She did not scream, yell or cry but simply stared out from under her bed, clutching the bear close and wondering if she was going to live through the day.

The rumble of the plane's engines gradually died down as the American Bomber Girls turned for home, mission accomplished. Then there was the all too familiar 'all clear siren'. The little girl slowly slid from her hiding place. She tiptoed across the room toward the door still cling on to her bear and dragging her blankets behind her. She was careful so not to cut her bare feet on the broken glass. All was quiet. When she opened her bedroom door…she found her apartment building was gone.

Surprise attack on Essen (24)

¥

There were no other missions in December of 1943. The squadron needed time to recover from the previous flights and to be brought up to full strength. The group flew practice runs as far north as Scotland. Christmas was spent entertaining the children from the town of Cambridge. The American Bomber Girls showed off their planes and treated the families to a fine dinner with dancing and presents. The young girls from town could not believe women flew the planes. Many said they wanted to be pilots when they grew up just like the American girls. The American Bomber Girls missed America and their own families but knew that going home was impossible.

¥

With the new year came new hopes for a quick and speedy end to the war. The Squadrons of the USAAF were all up to full strength and ready to pound the Reich into submission.

The American Bomber Girls' first mission of 1944 was to fly back to Essen, Germany in the Ruhr Valley to bomb the Krupp Manufacturing Plant. The allies made frequent raids on the factory but Krupp rebuilt the plant with the use of slave labor. The American Bomber Girls again severely damaged the plant without losing a single plane.

In February, the girls' planes were outfitted with the 75 mm cannon and they flew a sortie against the port city of Wilhelmshaven which was just across the channel from Hardwick on the French coast. The port housed a marine base with 200 ships. Later in February, the

American Bomber Girls took an active part in the USAAF's 'Big Week'.

In the last week of February, 1944, the USAAF and the RAF launched 'Operation Argument'. (A very fitting name that defined how well the RAF got along with the USAAF) The operation was a series of massive bombing missions against Germany. The seven day campaign was nick named 'The Big Week'. The Bombing raids were directed against the German aircraft industry with the intention of drawing the Luftwaffe into decisive air battles.

In the beginning of '44, the USAAF received a number of long range fighters call the P-51 Mustangs. In addition, with the external drop fuel tank, the P-38 and the P-47 fighters along with the formidable P-51s could escort the heavy B-17s to their targets and back to base. With fighter escorts, the B-17 casualties were significantly reduced.

As a result of 'Operation Argument', the combined American and British losses were 350 bombers but through-out the remainder of the war, the German fighter squadrons stayed close to the large German cities and did not stray into outlying areas.

In March the American Bomber Girls returned to Mainz. There was much apprehension about going back there due to the losses they suffered the previous two times they bombed Mainz. They attacked at dawn with little opposition. In April, the American Bomber Girls bombed Pforzheim, Germany. The city was completely destroyed. The Germans complained that the town had no war related industry but it did supply parts to the factories.

On June 5, 1944, the American Bomber Girls flew the most important missions in their history. Their planes were converted to gunships and flew across the channel to shell railroad stations, tracks and locomotives. Then they blasted highways and bridges including all tank and military vehicle movements. After returning to Hardwick where they were refueled and rearmed, the ladies took off again. The ladies proceeded to shoot up air fields in Northern France. All the American Bomber Girls had an idea that something huge was about to happen after being once again refueled and rearmed at Hardwick before they flew their third mission of the day. No one wanted to say why their missions were so important. The following day, June 6th, was of course D-Day.

   In August of '44, Colonel Daniels had the great idea to send the girls back to the city of Wilhelmshaven hidden in a flight of B-17s bound for Berlin. The B-25s were converted to gunships with four 50 caliber machine guns and the 75 mm cannon in the nose. As the massive fleet of 660 heavies passed Wilhelmshaven over the English Channel, Captain Edwards dropped under the armada much like fighters instead of bombers and dove on the port city taking it by surprise.

   The Germans did manage to muster some Me-109s from neighboring airfields but they were confronted by Commander Bowie and her P-38s. The air battle was short and Cyndy smiled as she watched a German pilot bail out of his burning bird.

CHAPTER 29

LIEUTENANT BETSY CARSON

Cyndy's celebration was short lived, for off to her port side the Commander could see a P-38 gracefully gliding toward the ground. Its starboard engine was dead and belching thick black smoke like a factory chimney. The pilot was Lieutenant Betsy Carson or 'BC' as she was affectionately called. Betsy did not appear to be in a whole lot of danger. She maintained level flight with one good engine but the plane was quickly losing altitude. Cyndy monitored Betsy's decent until her own plane was jumped by two 109s and she had to defend herself.

Betsy was the best wing woman in the squadron with seven kills and six assists. In addition, she seemed to revel in strafing targets on the ground such as fast moving locomotives or parked fighter planes on a German air field. When she could not find a suitable target, she would create one by shooting up a fishing boat, moving automobile or even farm houses. One afternoon she strafed a farm house. Her shells tore huge holes in the plaster exterior with no results. The aviatrix was persistent and would blast the next three houses with similar results. When she shot up the fifth house it disintegrated into a cloud of fire and smoke. *'Well, what do you know,'* she thought to herself. She always smiled and said 'Being a fighter pilot was not only about shooting down planes and escorting bombers.'

In addition, she was a top notch pilot. When she was in the cockpit, the plane and she were as one. No one could make an aircraft do the maneuvers that Betsy did so effortlessly. It was as if her bright silver P-38, 'The Man Eater,' could read its pilot's mind and it reacted well to her touch on the yoke.

Betsy was afflicted with a rare crippling disease that attacked the nervous system and she could have a seizure at anytime. She was a 5'3", blue-eyed, fair skinned, thin lady with straight brown hair. The 23 year old from Omaha, Nebraska, obtained her pilot's license when she 18 but it was taken away from her due to her condition. Before joining the 366th, all she had to look forward to was eventually being bed ridden and dying a long…slow…drawn-out horrible death. But Colonel Daniels appreciated the girl's flying skills so he gave her a P-38 fighter and had since been very happy with his decision.

Betsy was losing altitude and airspeed so she had to quickly find a flat surface to land. From her starboard window the pilot spotted a hayfield, a perfect place to set down the giant fighter. She waited until the last second before throwing the stick hard to starboard steering the plane toward the clearing. The maneuver reduced her airspeed and while her stall speed indicator began to scream, Betsy landed the 38 flat and level. She opted for a belly landing anticipating that a wheel would find a gopher hole that would flip the war bird upside down onto the cockpit. Still the aviator expected a bumpy ride.

The landing was not quite as bad as she expected. After the plane gently slid to a stop, Betsy quickly unbuckled her harness. She did not feel the throb of red hot pain in her left shoulder until she threw open the canopy using both hands. After making a yelping noise, she saw blood oozing from a tear in her flight suit between her left shoulder and chin. Betsy figured that in all the excitement she must not have felt the bullet hit her arm. Her shoulder began to ache as she slid down the side of her plane to the muddy earth below her feet. The port turbine of the twin tailed war bird began to pop and crackle throwing sparks in the air. Betsy knew that an explosion was imminent so she ran to the edge of the field and ducked behind a fallen log. From her vantage point, she witnessed her beloved aircraft begin to burn. Betsy felt she had lost her best friend.

Also burning was her shoulder. Betsy tore open her suit to examine the wound. Without her med kit, she could not clean up the cut. She remembered once lying in a hospital bed in pain and there was nothing anyone could do for her. She was only too eager to accept the assignment when approached by Col. Daniels.

The aviatrix was awakened from her fugue state by the gruff voice behind her. Slowly turning around, she was facing nearly a dozen Wehrmacht soldiers with their rifles leveled. Betsy didn't react but sort of stared at the Deutschers before raising her right hand above her head.

"Easy there Fritz," said Betsy.

The guy in charge (Betsy was not familiar with German uniform insignias so she didn't know his rank) said something to her in his language. She didn't understand the man.

The German growled something at Betsy so she calmly lowered her right hand under her bleeding shoulder and gingerly removed the colt .45 from its holster with her thumb and fore finger and tossed the side arm into a puddle. The Germans did not move but stared at the American girl, then looked at each other.

No one said anything for a few moments until the Germans spoke to each other in their tongue.

"You boys gonna sing the 'Star Spangled Banner' or get on with it?" demanded Betsy.

A large German pulled Betsy's legs out from under her dragging the girl on her back onto the wet muddy ground. The solders were clumsy as they struggled to strip the girl of her shoes, her shearling jacket, her flight suit and then all her undergarments. She laid on the ground with her arms folded across her bare chest.

"Don't you guys buy a lady dinner first?" asked Betsy with a small grin as she struggled with the much larger men. Don't misunderstand; Betsy was scared however she was not going let those guys know it. The American girl felt that hiding her fear would give her an edge over her captors. The women talked about being captured and assaulted while in their barracks at night. They wondered how they were going to act if it ever happened to them. It is kind of like jumping off the high dive at a swimming pool. One talks about not having a problem doing it until he/she is at the top of the ladder starring down at the water below.

A soldier on Betsy's left and right flank pulled her naked legs toward her chest while the first German soldier undid his pants and lowered them to his knees. Betsy leaned forward to see that the soldier was just a young boy of perhaps 16. He was a year older than her brother. She knew if she had relations with the boy, he would be dead in three months.

Betsy began to struggle. She did not sign on to this program to kill children. To actually say anything would betray the whole master plan and every one of her comrades would die for nothing...but then she looked at the young boy.

The German soldiers thought that Betsy was struggling so not to be raped not realizing that she was trying to save the boy's life. His comrades were holding their enemy down so she could kill their comrade. This war was becoming way too complicated. Betsy quietly lay on her back breathing hard, while two soldiers pinned her arms in the mud under their knees. The youth entered her. She may have been his first. She will most likely be his last.

The American girl did not make much noise or move much as the soldiers patiently waited for their turn. She let her mind wander to better times before the terrible disease took control of her life. She was from Nebraska. As a girl, she and her friends stole her mother's vodka one summer day and went skinny dipping at the old rock quarry near her home. She recalled how she got plowed but managed to return home and crawled into the lower rack of the bunk beds in her room. Betsy slept through the night but in the morning she sported a hangover that would cripple a bull elephant.

The Germans made jokes, pointed and laughed at their American prisoner. As the next few soldiers had their way with her, Betsy stopped struggling with her captors and relaxed. She found the molestation easier with each violation and she found it easier when she pictured each violator dying a horrible death in the next three or so months. The fifth one was very confused and the other

Germans stopped laughing when they noticed Betsy sort of grinned and chuckled as the man entered her.

After the first six soldiers had their way with Betsy, she rolled over on her stomach tucking her knees up under her nude body. The next German in line pulled her toward him by her waist. Betsy held up one finger, "Wait a sec," she exclaimed breathing heavy, "I need a minute."

The German did that understand and wrestled with the American girl who simply hunkered down on her knees resisting the large Deutcher. Just then another German intervened. He said something to the rest of the men who all backed away from Betsy. The weather had turned colder and a mist of rain began to fall as Betsy sat up on her heels with her arms wrapped around herself. She held her head up but she was shivering.

The German soldier had gone back to the half-track and returned with two blankets which he laid out flat on a grassy patch. He dropped to his knees on the blankets, unbuttoned his coat and pulled the girl close to him. He wrapped his oversized coat around the two of them before buttoning up the coat. Betsy felt warm.

The other soldiers pointed at the couple, said something in their tongue and laughed until the courteous German snarled at his comrades. From his coat pocket he produced a flask. After opening it he offered the girl a drink. Betsy turned her head. Bewildered, The German took a swig off the bottle. She gazed up at his smiling face looking down on her and took a big gulp off the bottle.

Betsy felt the elixir clear her sinuses and then burn like hell as it flowed down her throat. She coughed, much to the amusement of the other soldiers. "What is it, Fritz?" she asked.

"Es ist schnapps," said the German.

"Schnapps!" said Betsy.

"Ya, schnapps."

Betsy took another big swig off the bottle and had the same reaction. "Man this stuff is rough," she said. The other Germans again smiled and laughed but more with the girl then at her.

Back in 1944, schnapps was not the delicious peachy liquor that one buys at the grocery store today. Back then, schnapps was sold at Lowe's next to the paint thinner. Real German schnapps tasted much like turpentine.

The German soldier holding Betsy went to put the flask away. "Hey hey. Where ya goin' with that?" asked Betsy.

The German was puzzled, but only for a moment, and then gave the bottle back to Betsy. She took it under the coat, uncorked it, and then choked down a big gulp off the flask. "Oh boy, this stuff doesn't get any better…how can you fellas drink this swill?" said Betsy, swallowing yet another large slug of the burning booze. She closed her eyes and the German allowed her to catch about 12 minutes of sleep.

The hour was becoming late and the weather was turning cool. The German cradling the naked American girl gently shook her awake. He said something in his tongue that she understood to be 'Time to complete the mission.' The German unbuttoned his coat and Betsy flopped on her back on the blanket pulling the excess blanket over her shoulders to her waist. The soldiers did not take much interest in Betsy's breasts.

The last three men were quick. They probably were short of time or wanted to get out of the cold too. The German who cared for the American did not partake in the molestation of the girl. He fumbled with her flight suit and jacket as he helped Betsy put her clothes back on. To arrive at their post with a nude female flyer would bring down all kinds of trouble so it was in their own best interests to dress the lady. Betsy was happy that the kind Kraut could live a little longer anyhow.

When Betsy tried to stand, her gut cramped up. She let loose a loud moan and crumbled to her knees sitting on her ankles quietly murmuring. One of the soldiers lifted her face up by her chin, but she shook from his grip. Another soldier said something and laid the blankets one atop of the other on the grass. Betsy was laid on the blankets on her back. The edges were rolled up, giving six soldiers a place to hold onto the blankets creating a stretcher to carry Betsy to the half-track.

The American girl was laid on the floor of the truck while the soldiers climbed into the vehicle flanking Betsy on both sides. The trip was short but extremely bumping and Betsy's head hit against the floor a few times. The base the Germans brought her to was not a P.O.W. camp but an army base.

When the truck stopped, one man went into the Komandant's office while the rest of the men jumped out of the back of the truck and scattered in different directions, all except for the one soldier who care for the American girl in the field. He sat next to Betsy. Her stomach ached and her head hurt. The soldier held her hand in an attempt to comfort her. Suddenly and without warning, Betsy aspirated into one of her seizures.

The German freaked out staring at Betsy as her body tensed up and started to violently shake and bounce on the metal bed of the truck. She turned her head and bazooka vomited on the German's boots. The attack was short lived allowing the German to calm down and yell for one of his comrades to get a doctor. The doctor was too late. Betsy laid still on the floor of the truck with her eyes staring off into space. The Doctor climbed into the back of the truck and examined the American. Betsy had passed.

Betsy's German friend freaked out again. He had seen his friends die in combat but not like Betsy. He ran away behind a building, sat in the dirt, put his head in his hands and began breathing hard. He sobbed some striving to settle down.

Betsy was taken to the edge of the camp and laid to rest in a grave next to fallen soldiers. The Germans kept excellent records that have been recently put on the internet. They recorded the name, rank and serial number of all prisoners. The records included the prisoner's height and weight along with hair and eye color. The paperwork stated when and where they were captured and recorded when they died, if applicable. In addition, the German soldier sent a letter home to Betsy's family (it actually went to Col. Daniels) through the Red Cross telling how brave she was when she passed away.

¥

While digging through the archives, I found Lieutenant Betsy Carson's file as well as the paperwork for better then most of the American aviatrixes. The story of her capture and demise was well recorded by the

Germans, Americans and the Swiss Red Cross. I sort of filled in any missing details.

    An American Army officer went to Lieutenant Betsy Carson's home and presented her parents with the Distinguished Service Cross. When they wanted to know why their daughter received the award, all they were told that it was 'because of Lieutenant Betsy Carson's tremendous sacrifice for her country.' She passed away on October 28th, 1944…just three days from her 24th birthday. Her parents were very confused and the officer left without providing any answers.

CHAPTER 30

COMMANDER CYNDY BOWIE

"There is no argument, Commander. I'm grounding you! In your current state, over exertion can make you gasp for air and pass out, not to mention the G- forces you encounter in a P-38 will knock you into three weeks."

"Doctor, you have already grounded half my squadron. Without me the 366th will cease to exist. Not going to happen!"

"What am I to do, Commander? I can't let you fly. You don't even meet our minimal standards. You will crash."

Commander Bowie thought quietly for a moment. "What about surgery, Doc?"

"I'd have to slice you open from fore to aft, Cyndy. You have done your duty. You are the bravest of all P-38 fighter pilots. You have known this day was coming. There is nothing more you can do."

"So, what are my options?"

"You can go home and lie in bed for the next six weeks heavily medicated. Or stay in England and lie in bed for the next six weeks heavily medicated."

"What if I'm not heavily medicated so I could move about?"

"You will not want to move about. If you are not medicated, you will lay in bed screaming in pain! Maybe you should go home and be with family. Or do what I would not have the balls to do. Cyndy, if I were a fighter ace…I would not die the way I described!!"

"I don't have many options," said a solemn Commander.

Cyndy went to her room on the air base. She laid in bed but sleep did not come. *'Why can't I fly? I feel fine,'* she thought to herself. *'I wish I could get up there one more time…I would not come back down.'* Then an idea struck her brain like a P-38 Lightning bolt. *'Or do what I would not have the balls to do. Cyndy, if I were a fighter ace…I would not die the way I described!!'* "Oh that is what the doctor meant. That is what he was not trying to tell me" said Cyndy.

The next morning the Commander called her remaining fly girls for a conference. Twelve pilots showed up; of them, only five were fit to fly.

"Ladies, I have been grounded." Those in the room moan in agony from the news that their leader lost her wings. "There was a day our planes filled the sky," said Cyndy, "now, this is all that's left." The room was silent with the exception of the couple who had trouble breathing and gagged on their own phlegm.

"I've given this some thought and I am NOT going to take this lying in bed for six weeks waiting to die. We are all great pilots, the best the Air Force has to offer. We have been shot at, wounded and we have watched our friends die. They died doing what they loved, not lying on their backs screaming but screaming in a glorious death after killing Krauts.

"I've decided that is the way I'm going out. Not with a sniffle but a roar. The B-17s of the 764th bomber group is flying to Bremen in the morning. I intend to procure a P-38 and fly escort to the target."

"Commander, let me get this straight…you are planning to steal a P-38 off the line and fly escort to Bremen?" asked a pilot.

"Not just any 38, but I'm stealing my 38, 'The Hun Hunter'."

"Commander," piped up one of Cyndy's pilots, "A 38 can not make it to Bremen and back on a single tank of fuel."

"I know, Lieutenant." said Cyndy. Once again the room was silent while the flyers comprehended what their leader was saying.

"Commander, anyone who tries to make that flight will crash!" said the same pilot.

"I know, Lieutenant," replied Cyndy.

"We could flame alot of Krauts first," said the Lieutenant.

"Yes we will," said Commander Bowie.

The Lieutenant stood up and clapped her hands, "Let's do this!" she said with a smile.

"I'm in," said another flyer.

By the end of the meeting, Cyndy had eight able bodied women ready to fly with her to Bremen.

¥

The ground crew of the 366[h] worked through the night readying the P-38s to join the 764th later the next day. The crews crammed as many shells as they dared into the magazines and topped off the fuel tanks. The 764th was a squadron of 360 B-17 heavy bombers flying to Bremen to destroy the heart of Germany's war factories. The

British had pounded the city the night before… the Americans were going to finish the job.

It was early afternoon when Commander Bowie and her pilots casually and quietly climbed into their 38's. They fired up the twin Allison V-1710 engines and taxied out to the runway. "This is tower to P-38 1030…you do not have permission for take off…please return to the hangers."

"This is flight 1030…we are taking off so please clear us some sky."

"This is General Thomas…Bowie, return to the hanger now!!"

"Not gonna happen Hard Dick!" Cyndy throttled up as she and three other P-38's took off abreast of one another followed by a second wave of four fighters. In seconds Commander Bowie's small squadron was airborne.

"Commander Bowie, bring those planes back now and I may not court-martial you," screamed the General.

Cyndy switched her radio to channel two to communicate with her planes. "Red Fox to all Foxes, the 764th should already be airborne; we know the rendezvous point so maintain radio silence 'till we get there."

P-47 Thunder Bolt

Due to a navigation error and some misinformation from the source that gave Cyndy the rendezvous point, the Commander was late in catching up with the heavies. There was a squadron of 40 Republic P-47 Thunder Bolt fighter planes already escorting the B-17s. The P-47 was a large and heavy fighter overpowered by a Pratt & Whitney R-2800 Double Wasp radial engine that produced 2300 horsepower. The plane was 34 feet long with a wing span of 36 feet. It was well armed packing eight 50 caliber machine guns, four mounted on each wing root. The maximum speed of a P-47 was 433 MPH.

"This is Captain Ed Craven. Come in P-38s!"

"'Fast' Eddy is that you?" responded Commander Bowie.

"Hey ya Cyndy. No one said you would be joining us."

"You know how we girls are…all dressed up and no where to fly to. We thought we would smoke a few Krauts (I met a guy named Krautz in Ft. Myers once). What's that dark cloud in front of the bombers."

"Those are your Krauts, Cyndy."

"Why don't they attack, Ed?"

"They know this is the point my squadron is out of fuel and has to turn back. This point right here. They are waiting for us to break formation."

"So they are going to just sit there until you and your planes head back to base."

"Afraid so. They have learned that if we want to get back to England, we can go no farther than right here."

"Well they are in for a major surprise when we hit 'em!"

"Cyndy, you can't take on that many fighters with what just eight planes?"

"You watch me. Red Fox leader to Foxes, we will climb above them. When the Germans are distracted attacking the heavies we will swoop down out of the sun and chop them up. Gotta go Eddy."

The P-38s gained altitude in formation. Their numbers had swollen from eight to 20 because Captain Craven and a dozen of his pilots opted to fly with the 366th. "Eddy what are you doing, you don't have fuel for this?"

"No I do not…but we have decided to join in on the fun…maybe a sub or surface ship will pluck us out of the English Channel."

From their altitude, the Americans could see the German fighters attack the B-17's. "What kind of planes are those? I don't recognize them," mauled Cyndy aloud.

"Those are older Heinkels. I thought they were obsolete. They are not a big threat to a 38 or 47."

"Red Fox leader, let's get in and get hits. Use short bursts and stay with the heavies…no chasing the Germans."

Commander Bowie's squadron caught the unsuspecting German flyers off guard. The Americans stayed in formation and chopped up 19 enemy planes in the first pass, then broke into pairs to encounter the remaining Germans. "The Germans are flying so strangely. One just turned into my fire," noted one of Cyndy's flyers.

"They're rookies," said another.

"Well the way they are flying…they are not going to be around much longer."

"I just blasted another. The hell these guys are nothing but machine gun fodder," laughed one of Eddy's pilots.

The American fighters had no trouble staying in formations of two or four planes. The Heinkels 112s were 100 MPH slower than the 38's. After a short dog fight, a few Germans attempted one more counter attack but were quickly dispatched. "Cyndy, we gotta fly," said Eddy, "Good hunting."

"Be carful 'Fast' Eddy," said Cyndy.

"See you back at base! I'll take you out for a steak dinner."

'No you won't,' thought Cyndy, "Sure Ed, until then," she said.

Commander Bowie and her small flight stayed with the huge four engined B-17 bombers to the target. The B-17 pilots could see Cyndy's planes but maintained radio silence until the flak started when the 17s started their bomb run.

"Red fox leader to all Foxes, climb to 36 000 we will wait for the 17s to complete their bomb run. Try and conserve fuel."

The 17s dropped their bombs right on target a railway station used as a hub for troop movements. The mission was a success. The tracks and trains were made into scrap metal. In addition, two other targets of opportunity were struck.

When Commander Bowie rendezvoused with the 764th, the bombers had lost three planes due to flak. Cyndy and her pilots were tired but ready to encounter fighters on the way back to their air base and the 764th were happy to see them.

"Red Fox leader to all Foxes, watch for bandits."

The flight did not have long to wait. "Bandits, bandits two o'clock," said a lieutenant.

"Those are Messerschmitt 109s this time," said another.

"Hold your fire until they are close," said Cyndy.

The Me-109s made a pass firing their four MG-17 machine guns but did not hit anything. On their next pass Commander Bowie and her eight 38s broke into four pairs encircling the 17s like linemen protecting their quarterback.

Cyndy's girls opened up on the Germans. "I got one," reported one pilot when a Me-109 turned to a cloud of smoke.

"Me too," said another. "He's spinning toward Earth and I don't see a parachute.

"Kiera's been hit and she's going down," said an American girl. "C'mon Kiera jump, jump." Kiera did not get out.

Then the worst happened, an undamaged 38 spiraled toward the ground. The long fight was too much for the ill pilot. "Here they come again," said Cyndy. "And there are alot of them."

The sky was full of Messerschmitts. Cyndy could not figure out were all these planes were coming from. Her intelligence report said that Bremen had only 22 Me-109s assign to protect it. Cyndy's squadron did their best to stay grouped together but they were out numbered four to one. "I got one on my tail," reported one of Cyndy's pilots just before her starboard turbo exploded.

The small group of American women stayed with the bombers. The incoming Messerschmitts were more focused on shooting down the heavies than the 38s so the Germans only engaged an American fighter when they had no choice. The Germans were good pilots but so were Cyndy's pilots proving themselves by reducing the

German squadron. However, Commander Bowie was powerless to stop her pilots from crashing one at a time.

"I'm out of gas," reported Cyndy, "I'm going down."

"I'm out of bullets," said her wing-woman Alice. "But the Germans are breaking off their attack and heading for home."

"Head back to base. I'm going to set my plane down," said Cyndy."

"You betcha, Commander. Maybe a sub or surface ship will pluck me out of the channel. It's been great flying with you, Commander Cyndy."

"You too, Alice."

Commander Bowie found a paved road between some farmed fields. Even though her engines sputtered, she successfully made a fine landing before taxiing the plane to a stop. Cyndy needed a moment to catch her breath gasping for air because setting the plane down on a smaller than normal landing strip was also taxing.

The American girl unbuckled her safety harness. Before scampering out of the cockpit, she reached into a side compartment and took out two hand grenades stored there for just such an occasion. Cyndy slide down to the ground pulled the pins on the grenades and tossed them into 'The Hun Hunter' before she took off running. The two ensuing explosions set the large silver war bird on fire igniting the fumes in the empty gas tank creating a much larger inferno.

The Commander proceeded to dash through a wheat field toward a stand of 50 foot tall chestnut trees on the edge of the field. It was October and the evening was clear and the air was cool so when she reached the safe confines in the trees, the girl collapsed into the newly fallen leaves under the high tree. Her chest hurt as she gasped for a breath just like the doctor said she would. The smell of the rotting leaves reminded her of when she was younger playing in the woods around her New York state home.

    After a short respite, Cyndy heard German voices. Then suddenly a bullet fired from a Mauser peeled the bark from the tree she was under. The Commander peaked around the tree to see over a dozen German soldiers attempting to flank her.

    The American pulled her Colt .45 from its holster, rolled on her stomach and waited quietly for the first Germans to approach. She could hear them talking as they snuck through the tall old trees. Cyndy took a quick peek around the tree she was hiding behind and saw three soldiers drawing near her position.

    Cyndy exhaled sharply then flung herself before the oncoming Germans. She fired twice hitting the closest attacker in the chest. The first bullet would have killed him; the second round was for good measure. A German did not aim but fired his Mauser from the hip. The bullet ripped through Cyndy's jacket grazing a rib before exiting.

    Cyndy fired back hitting the German square in the chest. He was dead before he hit the ground. Then she shot at the third soldier who was just a kid. He did not move, frozen and bewildered. The bullet entered his head just above his nose, exited through the back of his head, ricocheted off the strong metal helmet reentering the boy's head before exiting out the top of the head and once again ricocheting then passed through the soldier's skull before finally exiting out of the boy's eye. The young soldier fell down dead.

The Commander knew the other soldiers were going to be looking for her and she felt running was not an option so the American woman scurried to the dead soldiers. Lying on the ground, she dragged one of the soldiers over her and then covered herself with dry leaves.

The Germans quietly encroached on Cyndy's hiding place. She could hear them whispering but they spoke in their tongue so Cyndy had no clue what they were saying so she silently waited. The seconds seemed like hours, one of the soldiers checked on the condition of his comrade. He glanced over at Cyndy but did not see her. Then his eyes suddenly grew large, wide open when he realized that the American flyer was hiding in the leaves.

The Commander shot the soldier point blank and he fell away dead. She rose to her knees and killed another German before two of the remaining soldiers machine gunned the girl in the chest. She fell back onto the ground in the leaves with her pistol by her side.

Cyndy opened her eyes to see four German soldiers hovering over her. The Germans were extremely puzzled when she smiled, laughed, and said, "Still beats the hell out of lying in bed screaming for six weeks!"

¥

None of Commander Bowie's P-38s returned home that day. The 764th only lost five planes from their fleet thanks to Cyndy and her flight. The Germans loss 62 fighters. Hermann Goring, leader of the German Air Force, said '…they had a bad day.'

'Fast' Eddy issued a Mayday once he and his flight of 12 P-47s cleared the French coast. After they ran out of gas, they had to ditch their planes in the English Channel. Lucky for him, a British sub was patrolling the coast and pulled Ed and his comrades from the cold waters. In a briefing later that day he regaled his story of Commander Cyndy Bowie and her lost squadron.

A few days later, a uniformed man knocked on the door of Cyndy's parent's home in Peekskill, New York. He explained their daughter was a hero and died in the line of duty defending her country from the Nazi Reich. Then the officer presented them with a Distinguished Service Cross for their daughter's bravery.

Cyndy was heralded as one of the American top aces of the war. In addition to her 10 kills and four assists, she flew 42 escort missions and was credited with severely destroying the German infrastructure.

CHAPTER 31

'THE ANGRY ALBATROSS' FINAL MISSION

As the women filed past their B-25s on a chilly morning in November of 1944, they paused to watch as once again their war birds were being converted from bombers to gun ships. "Here we go again," said Marie who did not like being forced into the nose loading and unloading the 75 mm. All she had to see out of the plane was a small window instead of the big Plexiglas bubble she enjoyed so much.

After the women were all seated and they quieted down, Colonel Daniels once again pulled open the curtain in front of the briefing hall displaying the now ever so familiar huge map of France and Germany. "Ladies," he started, "the gunship attacks have proven to be very successful. Today we need you to spearhead an attack on Ulm, Germany.

"Ulm is in the southeast of Germany. You shouldn't have any trouble finding it. Our objectives are the two truck factories there and a Wermacht barracks. We have ignored the town throughout the war so your attack should be a surprise to the Germans. There are few fighters assigned to Ulm and even fewer anti-aircraft guns."

Colonel Daniels went on to explain how the route of the B-25s would be through the newly liberated portion of France, close to Switzerland. It was to be a long flight, nearly three hours but the American Bomber Girls should not find any resistance until they were inside of Germany. Good thing because the flight would not have any air cover. The gunners will have to shoot straight this time. Daniels dismissed the girls.

"The Army must be running out of targets for us to hit such a small town," said Honey.

"If we are not careful, we may destroy the whole village," said Marie.

"Hey Captain, while we are there, can we stop and pick up one of them Ulm Black Forest cuckoo clocks for my mother?" asked Virginia.

"Very funny ladies," said Jennifer, "there is too much adlibbing going on. All I want is to fly to a German city, destroy it, and fly home! Is that to much to ask of my crew?"

"Ok Capt. We're sorry," said Honey as she slid into the hatch under the plane.

After going through the checklist, Jennifer once again fired up the small twin engine bomber and in no time all 36 planes were in the air. They climbed to 24,000 feet where they would stay for the long flight. Virginia did her due diligence and continued to monitor their position during the flight.

The flight was without incident. The crew saw a small squadron of German fighters a few thousand feet below them. The fighters either did not see the bombers or did not want to tangle with the B-25s…they simply flew on by. "Captain from Navigator, target in 20 minutes," Virginia finally announced.

"Alright every one, time to get sharp and call out those bandits when you see them," said Jennifer.

"Pilot from Navigator, you should see the town by now Jennifer."

"I sure do Gini. Fox leader to Foxes," announced Jennifer, "follow me down to 50 feet. We will attack the barracks first in four waves of nine. Let's do this just like we practiced it ladies."

The American planes found the sleepy barracks exactly where Virginia said they were supposed to be. The war birds swooped down on the unsuspecting camp like a flock of chicken hawks pouncing on a hen house. The American Bomber Girls let loose with their four 50 cals severing and mangling barracks, vehicles. Jennifer then punctuated the onslaught with the 75 mm cannon destroying buildings and supply huts.

The wail of the air raid siren was much too late. The soldiers scrambled for cover in all directions as the second wave of hawks continued to batter the base. The 75 mms ignited fuel tanks creating huge bursts of flames that licked the bottom of the planes. By the time Captain Lukka led the forth wave in; there was little left to blast. Her planes shot up supply trucks and found a few tanks running from the camp.

"Bandits, bandits, 12 o'clock high," shouted top turret gunner Lt. Sandy O'Malley into the intercom. She cocked the bolt of her twin 50 caliber machine guns as a squadron of four Me-109s dropped out of the sun onto the American gunships. Sandy learned her trade well and practiced with her 50 cals often on her own. She managed to vaporize two of the four fighters quickly forcing the others to veer off course. "Ha, ha, ha, take that you filthy animals," laughed Sandy.

As if the fighters were not enough of a distraction from their mission, the anti-aircraft batteries commenced their barrage on the small gunships. "The third and forth groups deal with the fighters. Group two follow me. We are going to silence those guns," ordered Jennifer.

'The Albatross' lead the attack on the big guns with her 50 cals. The Germans hastily aimed and fired on the American girls. Their shells flew true and burst around the B-25. The fire did not hit the plane but the accuracy was enough to distract Jennifer when she misdirected the 75 mm to the right. Just before she flew over the big guns, a shell burst below the plane lodging a single small shard through the outer skin.

There were definitely fewer German cannons at Ulm but the batteries were the new RADAR guided anti-aircraft guns. The guns used target RADAR which automatically considered wind direction and type of shell used to calculate its aim point. These figures were electronic commands fed to the gun's hydraulics to point themselves at high speeds. By 1944, these advanced guns were in late development.

Jennifer was followed by a second war bird. The Gunners used the first plane to adjust their sights so they were deadly precise hitting the next B-25 directly on the 50 cal blowing off the front of the plane and sending it crashing into the populace below. Lukka attacked the guns at a low altitude hoping to fly below their sights. She was doing fine, firing a 75 mm shell into a gun battery sending fragments of the gun and crew in all directions. A large pine tree scraped the bottom of her plane sending her almost straight up giving a German battery an opportunity to get a fix on Lukka's plane. The big gun fired twice sending the two shells into Lukka's port fuel tank blowing her plane into dust.

The anti-aircraft battery got a fix on another B-25 and fired. The shell drove into the plane between the wings before detonating blasting the war bird and crew out of the sky. "We gotta do something Capt.," said Honey, "Those guns are killing us."

"I have an idea," responded Jennifer.

Jennifer hit the gas and flew to the edge of town at maximum speed before dropping to tree top level and coming up behind the guns. The Germans never saw what hit them when she pounded the big guns from behind with repeated 75 mm shells. The American Bomber Girl was successful in silencing the batteries but she was low on fuel. "Lead fox to all foxes. Time to head for home. Form up on the west side of town for the trip back to base."

Just as the group started on the long trip home, 'The Albatross' began to display engine trouble. "What's happening?" asked Honey.

"I don't know, we are losing power on both engines. One would not be strange but both? Something is terribly wrong."

"Were we hit? No one said we were hit," said Honey. Then the stall speed indicator began to scream. "We're going down, Capt."

"Captain to crew, we are going down. I'll hold her steady. Everyone bail out, bail out!!" said Jennifer calmly into the intercom, "You too Honey. I'll try and hold her steady."

CHAPTER 32

LT. MARIE TREMBLY & LT. SANDY O'MALLEY

"Captain to crew, we are going down! I'll hold her steady. Everyone bail out, bail out!!" said Jennifer calmly into the intercom, "You too Honey. I'll try and hold her steady."

Marie slipped into her parachute before dropping out of the hatch in the bottom of the plane in front of the bomb bay doors. Her chute deployed right away without incident and she drifted safely toward Earth. The winds were in the Canadian girl's favor taking her south and west away from the beloved airplane and the mayhem on the ground. Marie landed in a grove of pine trees caught on a branch dangling a few feet from the ground. She unbuckled the parachute harness, dropped the final six feet and then rolled just as she practiced in training. Instinctually, Marie drew her .45 and looked about to see that there was no one around.

While Marie made her way through the underbrush of twisted fallen limbs, she made a most unwelcome find. She found the port waist gunner of 'The Albatross', Teresa, dead. Teresa had also drifted south into the pine tree forest but a broken bough had caught her chute and impaled the American Bomber Girl through the chest.

"Oh Teresa," said Marie aloud, "No!"

Marie tried to free Teresa but her attempt was futile. Teresa was much larger than Marie and well stuck over the Canadian's head. "I'm so sorry Teresa," said Marie when she realized that there was nothing that could be done. "The Germans will give you a decent burial."

Marie had to get moving. She went south toward Switzerland. While staying off the main road she was successful at eluding capture. There was not much traffic anyhow…no military vehicles or anything else. Night fell but Marie pressed on as long as she could utilizing the darkness to conceal her movements. Eventually fatigue overcame the girl and she found a place to curl up and sleep until morning.

When Marie woke, the sun was already warm. She was hungry, thirsty and wished she had not forgotten the survival kit before falling from the plane. At least Marie had a map and a compass. She turned south and west a more direct route to Switzerland and a better chance of going home. Switzerland interned American flyers for the duration of the war. The internment camps were much more comfortable than a German prison camp. Because Marie was a woman, there was a very good chance the Swiss would repatriate her to Canada.

The hunger began to gnaw at Marie's stomach. Finally she found a farm. With a vantage point above the farm house she could watch the farm for a while to see who came in and out. There was an old couple and no one else around. Marie observed the house for nearly an hour.

'Time to make my move,' Marie thought to herself.

The farmer went into the barn leaving the old woman alone in the house. Marie quickly and quietly sneaked into the open barn door and came up behind the old man with her gun drawn.

"Hey," said Marie.

The startled farmer turned toward the uniformed girl. "Englander," he croaked.

"Actually, I'm from Canada. Look, I don't mean you any harm," explained Marie, "I need food and drink then I will go."

Marie could tell that the farmer did not understand. He said something in German with a nasty threatening tone and then slowly stepped over to a pitch fork hanging on the wall.

"No, no, don't do that old man," said Marie shaking her head. "I'll shoot!"

The farmer faced Marie with the pitch fork posed at her chest saying something in his tongue.

"Put it down!" Marie ordered. The old man slowly approached her. "Damn it man, stop or I will shoot!"

Just as the situation could not be any more tense, the farmer's wife stepped into the doorway and she screamed at the sight of the girl. Marie's attention was distracted from the farmer. The old man lunged at Marie narrowly missing her with the pitch fork. Marie's reflexes were sharp and she nested two shots into the man's face. Then she turned and pumped three slugs into the woman's chest. Marie didn't mean to fire that many times…it was as if the gun went off by itself after the first shot.

"You stupid stubborn Krauts! All I wanted was something to eat," Marie said aloud as if the dead couple could hear her.

Marie holstered her gun and went into the kitchen to help herself to bread and some dried wurst on the counter. Hot fresh strong coffee was on the stove. It helped Marie feel a little better. After looking around the courtyard outside of the kitchen door, Marie found a small flatbed truck. She unloaded the hay piled in the back and then started it up. She checked the map before pulling out on the paved streets on her way to Switzerland.

The road to Switzerland was not long and without incident. Marie slumped down behind the steering wheel when a car or tractor came from the other direction. There was a German check point with a small gate across the road and two well armed guards at the border with Switzerland. The guards wanted Marie and her truck to stop at the gate. She slowed down to give the Germans a false sense of security before the girl stepped on the gas and sped towards the surprised guards.

As Marie approached the gate, she drew her .45 and started popping off at the Germans through the driver's side window. After the clip was empty, she set the gun on the seat next to her. The two German guards scrambled for cover as Marie crashed the front of the truck through the gate without any trouble.

The Swiss had a check point on their side of the border with no gate. The Swiss soldiers leveled their rifles. Marie tossed out the empty gun and put up her hands. She was taken into custody.

¥

The Swiss took Marie to an internment camp for Americans. They explained to her in French that they had just captured an American fly girl the day before and the two would be bunking together. When Marie found her room, Sandy O'Malley was lying on her bed with a hand on her chest.

"Sandy," said Marie, "are you ok? It's Marie."

Sandy opened her eyes and smiled at Marie. "Marie, I'm so glad you made it out of 'The Albatross'," said Sandy. "Did anyone else?"

"I found Teresa but she was dead. She is the only other one of our crew."

"No matter, Marie. I'll be joining them soon."

"Don't talk like that. What's wrong?"

"It's my heart. It was weak before but now with all the excitement of jumping from the plane and making my way here…it was just too much. And then there were these two Swiss soldiers who raped me before I was brought here. I tried to tell them not to but I did not want to risk the mission. The stupid asses probably thought I was struggling not to be molested when in fact I was trying to save their miserable lives. They will be dead in a few months. I have been lying here wondering if Colonel Daniels thought about that when they came up with this cockamamie scheme. Where you raped Marie?"

"No, they just brought me here; it wouldn't have made any difference."

Sandy sat up. "What do you mean by that?'

"Nothing, lay back down."

"You meant something or you would not have said it, Marie. Did you take the shot?" demanded Sandy.

"Sandy, I was not like the rest of you. Daniels hired me for my brains he told me so. I'm not sick and I had no intention of being sick. So I stuck myself with a needle in the arm to appear I took the shot. Unlike the rest of you, I have something to live for and that is to come out of the war alive."

"You betrayed the squadron," insisted Sandy.

"How? I had the best bomb pattern of anyone in the group including the men. We destroyed all those subs because of me. I served my country and yours." By the time Marie finished her rant, Sandy was dead. Her heart stopped beating and there was nothing anyone could have done for her.

Marie was sent home with Sandy's body courtesy of the Swiss Red Cross. Sandy's mother was able to give her daughter a nice funeral with friends and family before receiving a Distinguished Service Cross for Sandy's sacrifice.

Marie told her story to Colonel Daniels and it became a part of the 10th record. Marie went home with her Distinguished Service Cross, lived out the war. In 1947, she put a .45 in her mouth and pulled the trigger. She was clutching her medal at the time of her death.

CHAPTER 33

CAPTAIN JENNIFER EDWARDS AND LIEUTENANT HONEY BLAKE

"Captain to crew, we are going down! I'll hold her steady. Everyone bail out, bail out!!" said Jennifer calmly into the intercom, "You too Honey. I'll try and hold her steady."

Honey unbuckled her safety belt and made her way toward the exit under the bombardier's position. As the co-pilot was slipping into her parachute, she hesitated, and then returned to the co-pilot seat. "What are you doing, Lieutenant? I told you to hit the silk," said Jennifer.

"Not gonna happen, Capt. You're going to need my help setting the plane down," said Honey fastening her seat belt, staring at Jennifer with her green eyes. "Have you picked a spot to set her down?"

"There's a field on the horizon. I think we can use it."

"We goin' in wheels up, right Jenn?"

"Yeah, I guess that would be prudent. I really don't know seeing how I haven't crashed a Mitchell recently."

"Recently!?" asked Honey.

"The controls are getting sluggish. Sound off the airspeed and altitude while I hold her steady."

"Yeaaah, ok Capt."

As the field grew closer, Jennifer did not have to adjust the plane's airspeed. The wounded 'Albatross' fell from the sky with grace. She sort of lost air speed and power on her own before thick black smoke began to belch from the port engine.

"We are at 50 feet Capt," announced Honey. "40 feet. 30, 20"

"Full flaps," said Jennifer.

The Captain held the plane steady with the nose up until her stall speed indicator began to howl.

"85 miles an hour," said Honey.

At the last second, Jennifer dropped the nose into the wet dirt.

The war plane's landing was bouncy and bumpy tossing the two pilots in their seats like a couple of rag dolls. As it came to a halt, Jennifer had to catch her breath. "That wasn't so bad was it, Honey?" she said to the co-pilot. "We had best get out of here, that smoke could be seen for miles." Honey laid back in her seat. "Honey?" said Jennifer. She shook the co-pilot. Honey's head turned toward Jennifer and then blood ran down the side of the girl's face from under her aviator's cap. A bump tossed Honey's head up against the side window. Her large green eyes stared off into oblivion. Lieutenant Honey Blake passed away from her injuries. "Damn," said Jennifer quietly.

The plane sat level on the earth. All the usual escape hatches were buried under the weight of the war bird so Jennifer quickly inched her way through the empty bomb bay and then slid through the short tunnel into the waist gunner's compartment. There, she scampered out through the open window just to find a waiting farmer with his pitchfork aimed at the Captain's chest.

Jennifer raised her hands, "You speak any English there, Fritz?" she quietly asked.

The German said something in his tongue and the American girl just shrugged her shoulders. While the two stood like statues facing one another, an army truck with about half a dozen German soldiers pulled up. The soldiers filed out with their guns and after a short conversation with the farmer, they took Jennifer prisoner pulling her by the arm back to the truck trudging through the uneven dirt. The soldiers were not rude or harsh, but seemed as if they were trying to assist the Jennifer to their truck instead of dragging her by the arm.

Jennifer climbed into the back of the military truck, filed to the front of the covered truck bed and took a seat on the hard wooden bench. The soldiers all piled in the truck and it pulled out of the field. "Are you hurt?" asked one of the Germans in English.

"I'm a little sore, fine for now, but I'm going to feel the bumps in the morning," said Jennifer, somewhat surprised to hear English spoken.

The German smiled and offered her a bottle of schnapps and a wurst made of dried sausage. Jennifer turned it down. "What's wrong Captain?" the soldier politely asked, "Are you afraid I'll poison you? I'm just trying to be hospitable."

Jennifer accepted the German's food and drink after all it could be a while before she might eat again and she was not sure what was waiting for her, being a woman and all. She took a bite of the sausage before a big swig off the flask. "Whoa, what is this stuff?" she asked as her throat burned.

"You Americans don't like a strong drink!"

"Yeah we do. But we use this stuff to clean corrosion from battery terminals." Jennifer took another long gulp just the same.

The ride was short. Two of the soldiers politely helped Jennifer down out of the truck and escorted her to the office of the Kommandant. Jennifer looked around…she was not at a Prisoner-of-War (POW) camp but what looked like a training facility. There were soldiers in formation and marching with their Mausers. When she entered the outer office of the camp, she was received by the Kommandant immediately.

"Please come in," said the Kommandant cordially in English, "sitzen sie."

"I'll stand, danke," replied Jennifer.

"How was your landing?"

"Jennifer Edwards. Captain. 164716…164716…164715…just a second," she said, holding up a finger before digging under her shirt for her dog tags. "I have it, 16471597."

"You don't know your serial number?"

Jennifer shrugged, "I know where to find it."

The Kommandant laughed, "I am Kolonel Hans Decker. I wish you would sit down and have a little drink before we get to business," he said pouring Jennifer a tall wine glass full of something from a decanter.

Jennifer sat down in a high back padded chair. In her mind was a nagging thought about how she was going to complete her mission…kill Germans. "This is not that swill I had on the truck, is it?"

"No Captain, this is a spatlese from my own vineyard in the Rhine River Valley. I think you will enjoy it."

Jennifer took a sip and then another, "Now this is good stuff. So tell me Kolonel, do you treat all POW's this well or is it because I'm a woman?"

"You wish to come to the point. Not yet, Captain Edwards. Will you answer a few questions first?"

"Ok, shoot. No no, don't shoot I mean go ahead and ask."

"You make me laugh. It is hard to be mean to you."

"Try."

"Ok. Where is your air base?"

"That's easy…just outside of Berlin. My turn to pose a question, where is the rest of my crew?"

"Well, we found three dead women on the plane. They will be brought here for a proper burial. A Teresa Gallo was found dead in her parachute. Virginia White was captured and is on her way to a POW camp. That is all we found so far. I'm sorry for your loss of your crew members, Jennifer. I know how you feel being a pilot myself until a Russian fighter chewed up my Ju-88 bomber over Stalingrad. I was the lone survivor."

Jennifer put her forehead into one hand and under her breath chocked back a few tears trying not to allow the German to see how bad she felt about losing her ship and crew. She quietly finished the balance of her wine before holding up her glass for the Kolonel to refill it. After a short and uncomfortable silent few moments, an auxiliary stepped into the room with a tray of small German sandwiches. The Kolonel gestured for Jennifer to help herself; she did. "Kolonel, danke for the information about my people. You can wine and dine me all you want but I'm an American officer and will not tell you anything."

"You are a woman. And a very beautiful one too. You should understand that you are going to spend the rest of the war right here in this camp. No POW camp for you. I am not going to tell anyone you are here. You will stay here."

"You are not allowed to do that. I am an American officer and you have to obey the laws laid down by the Geneva Convention…"

"Hang the Geneva Convention! No one knows you are here I have listed you as dead with your crew. There will be no white knights coming to save you Captain."

"What do you want, Kolonel?"

"Again to the point, Jennifer. I'm not sure I like that quality in you. I want you to stay here and be my little lady, my partner and my possession."

"You mean your whore!"

"Jennifer, you should not look at it that way. You will be well treated. You will dress in pretty clothes, eat well and be well cared for. I like having parties here and you will help me entertain Generals from the High Command."

"You bucking for General yourself, aren't you, Kolonel?"

"You may be my only hope since I'm confined here at this camp to be a school teacher until the end of the war."

"Aren't you afraid that with me around…the end of the war could come quick and sudden for you?"

"Then the end would be just as quick for you!"

"What if I refuse?"

"You understand that you are never leaving this camp. Refuse me and I'll have you stripped and shared amongst the men until the end of the war."

"Wow Kolonel, you give me such great options…how can a girl choose?"

The Kolonel chuckled, "I have to admit, I so enjoy your American sense of humor. Take some time to think it over, you have three minutes."

"I don't need three minutes, I'll take the barracks," said Jennifer, feeling she could kill many Germans in a short time.

"You decided so quickly...shouldn't you think it over?"

"I have...I'll sleep with the men."

"We are having squab for dinner tonight."

"En...joy," said Jennifer smugly.

"You are a foolish little girl," said Kolonel Decker with a frown.

"Hey, no hard feelings, huh Kolonel."

"No my dear...none at all...GAURDS!" four young soldiers who were ever waiting in the outer office came in. "Strip her, then she is all yours."

Jennifer's eyes grew big as the four soldiers pounced on her like a cat on a mouse. They tore at her clothing much like the big cat would tear at its prey. Jennifer did not struggle. She figured that in the barracks, she would have an opportunity to sicken the whole camp. When the men finished disrobing her of her bra and even her shoes, Jennifer stood before them with her arms across her breasts a little embarrassed.

"Turn around for us Jennifer," ordered the Kolonel.

Jennifer did as she was told giving the Germans a good look at her. She was a beautiful, 5'10" tall, slender, with broad shoulders that tapered off into her slender waist then filled out at the hip. Her long wavy flowing brown hair hung to the middle of her back. She was older then most of the women in the group, 27, and at that time hoped to see 28. "Look all you want, I'm still going to the barracks!!" she exclaimed.

"Take her," instructed a most disgusted Kolonel, "You'll change your mind."

"Don't count on it, Kolonel."

Two of the men led a naked Jennifer across the compound to the first hut full of soldiers. When she stepped inside the American girl felt most uncomfortable. There were around 15 Germans in the barrack and all eyes were ogling Jennifer. One man close to her jumped down from his top bunk and ran his fingers up and down her bare chest.

"Tell the Kommandant I changed my mind," Jennifer whispered to one of the soldiers who brought her to the hut. "And do it quickly." Killing Germans is the mission…but she felt that this was over doing it just a bit. She was overwhelmed by looking at all those antsy men all wanting a piece of her…the lady decided that killing a few Generals was a better course of action.

Once again Jennifer was led away by two soldiers. The Kolonel anticipated Jennifer's change of heart and ordered the soldiers to take the naked American girl to another hut near the Kommandant's office. When she went inside, she found a very lush and lavish small apartment with nice furnishings. There was a beautiful old couch in the center of the room with ornamental legs and back. It looked like a remnant from the Louis the 16th collection. In addition to other old furnishings, there was an antique writing desk against the wall. Jennifer proceeded into the bedroom to find a large and again antique bed with a canopy, a matching dresser and credenza. In the closet was a variety of very pretty woman's clothes.

The apartment reminded her of the hospital room Jennifer's parents had arranged for her well-suited for her last days. Jennifer was quick to join the Army Air Corp when approached by Col. Daniels. Her mother could not even look at Jennifer without bursting out in tears.

So Jennifer was still naked, lost in her train of thought but was abruptly derailed by an extremely young lady who joined her in the bedroom. "Come," said the girl, taking Jennifer's hand and pulling her into the bathroom. The maiden had drawn Jennifer a hot bath and led the American girl to the tub. Jennifer just shrugged her shoulders and stepped into the tub of hot water then immersed her body in the bath. The young girl left Jennifer alone. Before long, Jennifer's eyes closed. She struggled to stay awake but the events of the day and the sadness of losing her plane and crew were way too much for her who fell into a deep sleep.

CHAPTER 34

JENNIFER PROCEEDS WITH HER MISSION

Jennifer felt someone holding a rag over her nose and mouth. She quickly woke and snatched the young girl, in her apartment, by the wrist. The girl was only using the cloth to wash Jennifer's face. She sorta took Jennifer by surprise. The girl was frightened and stood up to leave.

"No, wait," implored Jennifer. "Don't go. You startled me that's all." The girl was at the door. "Nein, come," said Jennifer beckoning. The young lady stopped and returned to the tub. "Sitzen sie, bitte," said Jennifer. The girl sat down on the same stool she was parked on a moment before. "Jennifer," said the American pointing at herself. "You?" she said pointing at the girl.

The girl thought for a second, "Hodl," she said. "Jennifer, Hodl," she repeated.

"Ya," said Jennifer with a smile. "Hodl, is that Deutsche?"

"Nein, Judisch."

"You're Jewish?"

"Ya, Judisch."

The Kolonel instructed Hodl to take care of Jennifer, to be Jennifer's servant. She was a very pretty girl but young. Jennifer did not ask her how old she was due to the complexity of the question. She figured Hodl to be only 14 or 15 years old. Jennifer also wondered if the

Kolonel was banging the young slave girl. *'He better not be,'* thought Jennifer.

Jennifer dressed in a pretty green dress with long sleeves and a vest to fend off the chilly afternoon air. Hodl poured her a glass of chilled Riesling before going through the swinging doors into the kitchen to fix themselves some dinner.

It wasn't long before there was a gentle rap on the door. Jennifer opened it to find Kolonel Decker. "Guten abend, herr Kolonel. Here to mount your new trophy already?'

Decker was obviously disgusted with the American girl's crassness. "No need to be rude Jennifer. I am only here to see how you are doing."

Jennifer was embarrassed, "Please come in, Kolonel."

Decker sat on the couch while Jennifer parked on the thick padded leather chair. Hodl fetched the Kolonel a glass of wine. He spoke to her in their tongue. "Ya Kolonel," said Hodl.

"Did you just send her to get champagne and caviar, Kolonel?" asked Jennifer.

"Yes, I did. I thought you don't speak German."

"I don't, but I do understand champagne and caviar. You live well here Kolonel."

"As will you Jennifer."

"Providing I do as I'm told like Hodl."

"Not like Hodl…but yes…you understand things."

"It's going to take some getting used to."

"I don't understand 'used to'," said the Kolonel.

"Accustomed to," explained Jennifer.

"Ah so. How do you find your quarters, Jennifer?"

"Satisfactory. There is a war on you know. Where did you find such elegant surroundings?"

"Courtesy of the United States Army Air Corp."

"Huh?"

"You bomb the hell out of our towns, killing our people and leaving their belongings scattered across the streets. I just pick and chose what I want."

"You're welcome, Kolonel."

"Bitte Jennifer, call me Hans."

"Sure Kolonel Hans."

That was about the time Hodl came back with a plate of cheese and crackers neatly arranged around a bowl of black fish eggs. Jennifer and Decker talked into the night until she informed the Deutscher that it was time for him to go.

¥

Jennifer quickly adjusted to her new role. She did not resist the first time Decker wanted to have relations with her…or the second or third time. Jennifer felt that Decker was as good as dead by then. Furthermore, she was able to seduce a German General away from one of Decker's parties and bang his brains out. That same evening a colonel wanted to slip away from the gathering. Jennifer obliged. *'He's a goner, too,'* she thought to herself. *'I guess I should keep score,'* she thought in her head. Decker was pleased with his little American trophy's performance and could see that red stripe on his pants (General uniform) already.

A month passed, the season changed, and the German winter was setting in. Decker gave Jennifer a longer leash allowing her to go into town to do some shopping for new clothes with a guard. Not a uniformed man, but a sergeant dressed in street clothes. While sipping coffee in a small café, she met some of the women from town. Jennifer enjoyed talking with them and they shared their wine and wurst with her. The German women never met an American before. "You will, soon!" insisted Jennifer. Life for Jennifer was not too bad but she was still a prisoner.

Then it finally happened. A crew of American flyers bailed out of their wounded B-26 Marauder. They were quickly rounded up by Kolonel Decker's men and brought to the camp. Jennifer was unaware that they were inside the gate as they were being unloaded from the half track. She was speaking English to Hodl not seeing the American airmen. To make matters worse Decker's Sergeant Carl who spoke English was leading them to the Kommandant's office.

"Hey, who is that girl?" demanded the captured American airman. "She speaks English, is she American?"

Jennifer froze not knowing what to do or say. "That's Jennifer," said Carl, "the Kolonel's girl."

"The Colonel's girl, huh?" said the flyer, "I see what's going on here! More like a collaborator. Who are you lady? Are you one of those 'American Bomber Girls' I've been hearing about? I bet you are and you are here collaborating with the enemy." Jennifer wanted to pull him aside and explain her mission but Colonel Daniels words about total secrecy resounded in her head. She mouth 'shut up' but the American who missed it.

"You're a traitor, a traitor and a whore. You sold yourself for free privileges. When I get back home I'm going to tell everyone about you. A fly girl betraying her country for favors you fucking little whore."

The Kolonel was just stepping down the stairs when he heard the end of the flyer's rant. He was obviously angered by the American's comment and felt no one could talk about his lady like that. He said something to the sergeant. The sergeant ordered the Americans to lineup. Jennifer knew what the Germans were planning.

"Please, Hans," it was not real often that Jennifer called the Kolonel Hans. "Please, Hans, don't do this. Punish them if you must but don't execute them…not for me. I can handle their talk but I do not want their deaths on my conscience."

"Halt," shouted Decker. "Jennifer, insulting you is the same as insulting me and all of Germany. By law, they must be executed."

The Americans stood still, sort of lax until an German auxiliary gave one a rifle butt to the gut. "Stand at attention," ordered Carl.

"Hans, I have done everything you have asked of me without ever asking for anything in return. Now I'm asking you nicely to find a suitable punishment for these men."

"Don't defend us you whore," said the American flyer.

"For the love of Pete, shut up! Ok, that one you can shoot…but not the others. You can do with them as you wish." With that said Jennifer turned and walked away. Not much later, she heard a single gun shot. She was sure she had her way.

Jennifer went to her apartment. She stepped inside and kicked off her shoes. After dropping her coat on the floor, the lady crashed into her couch. She quietly wept knowing that the American was right. Jennifer was conflicted. Compromising a few principles led to her chance to kill German generals hand picked by Hitler himself. Surely that would bring about a speedy end to the war, she thought to herself. *'Or am I just rationalizing to cover up that I have it so good while others have it so bad?'* "I can't think of this right now!" she said out loud. She closed her eyes and fell asleep.

That evening was frightfully cold. The surviving American airmen were stripped completely naked and made to stand at attention all night. Jennifer snuck out to talk to one. "I'm Captain Jennifer Edwards. I'm here on a special secret mission. I kill Germans. I saved your miserable ass," she told one of the flyers. "In return, I expect you guys will not say anything to anyone or I'll have you shot as an American traitor. Do we have an accord or do I have the rest of you shot at sun up?"

"We have an accord Miss. What do I care what you do."

"Sorry I could not save your Captain but he shot his mouth off in front of a German officer."

"Not to worry Miss, we all hated him anyway."

Jennifer quietly chuckled then looked between his legs. "They sure don't make fly boys like they use to."

"It's the cold Miss."

¥

Again, life for Jennifer was alright. She lived comfortably while the people in the towns she visited suffered from mild to severe shortages. After four months, she did her job well. Casualties of German officers due to illness rose. The Germans did issue a health warning about many deaths due to a strange virus in the area; however, there was limited discussion about it. Jennifer continued targeting generals but she was not above bopping a Colonel and a Major once in a while.

CHAPTER 35

HANS BREATHES HIS LAST

Kolonel Decker laid in his bed unable to suck in a healthy breath. The pneumonia had so filled his lungs with fluid that breathing became laborious. He was still in command of his camp; however, Major Kline was in charge of the day to day goings on. Kline replaced Major Schmitt who recently and mysteriously died of the flu even though he was a healthy young man. People thought it was strange that he died just two weeks after his young wife passed away leaving four children without parents.

Kolonel Decker laid in his bed ever convinced that his last days were upon him. He summoned Jennifer to his side for comfort. The German wanted to spend his last remaining days with his best friend and confidant. "Ah Jennifer, I'm so glad you came," said Decker when Jennifer came through the bedroom door.

"Again Kolonel, I have no choice. How you feeling, Hon?"

"Terrible. I can't breathe."

"I saw the doctor here. What did he say? Are you going to live, Kolonel?"

"To hell with the doctors, they can't even treat a bad cold."

"It's…pneumonia."

"Ya, I am told. Jennifer I am not going to make it through the night," complained Decker. He called for his aide. He told the aide that 'he was not to be disturbed.' Jennifer understood that much German being that she had heard him say it so many times. She saw a chance for some pay back.

"Don't talk like that Kolonel. Where is that tough Nazi spirit, 'Never say die' and all that other bullshit?"

Decker smiled at the American girl, "You always make me laugh. Of all the people I have met I could always count on you to be cheerful, happy and make me smile. You became your part here in my camp so well, never complaining or trying to escape. You are the only one I can count on.

"I can not guarantee your safety after I pass, Jennifer. I have left orders for you to be treated as my widow but I'm not sure the new kommandant will respect them. You know I have always thought of you as more than just my lady."

"That is nice of you, but well Hansy baby, here's the truth. All the American Bomber Girls and I were selected for a top secret mission. Our own families don't know were we are or what we are doing. All those letters you mailed to my mother for me, thank you very much, were reports to my commanding officer. They were in code of course."

"Nooooo," said Decker.

"Oh yes and there is more…lots more. After training to fly the army way, the girls were infected with a sexually transmitted disease. The bug was developed in a lab. It will not harm its host, least not right away but it will kill anyone who comes in contact with us. It kills quickly, usually in three to four months. Actually, I'm surprised you have lasted as long as you have. The disease is easily transmitted from one infected person to healthy person but only through intercourse. It attacks and destroys the victim's immune system making him powerless to fend off the simplest ailments or even pneumonia."

Decker's eyes grew larger as Jennifer told her tale. His smile disappeared from his face and replaced by panic. "You are catching on, good," continued Jennifer, "all those Generals you introduced me to and almost insisted I have sex with, are all goners. As well as the Colonels and Majors. There have been so many of them I've loss count. The best part of all of this is I have you to thank. I couldn't have done it without you."

"You whore," said Decker, trying to get up but only to be pinned down by the American girl's hand to his chest.

"Where do think you're going? I'm not done with my mission yet."

"Jennifer how could you?" asked Decker just dumfounded by Jennifer's tale.

"It was easy, you brought them here and I banged their brains out. They died. And hopefully they took a few more Germans with them."

"No, how could you do this thing after how well I treated you?"

"Treated me??? I'm an American Army Captain. You made me your whore. Now look at you, all your scheming is crashing down on your head…well actually your lungs. No worries though Kolonel …I will be joining you soon. You see, there is another reason I was chosen to be a Bomber Girl. I have this thing in my head eating away at my brain cells. Hell on my last flight with my 'Albatross', I missed half the preflight check list. My co-pilot Honey filled in the gaps for me. Getting captured was the best thing to happen to me because it gave me a chance to fulfill my destiny. Even now I have noticed the loss of many of my involuntary motor skills. Damn, I'm lucky I don't shit myself during the day. It won't be long before one night I will go to sleep and won't wake up. Until that time Hansy baby, I fully intend to kill Krauts."

"You will not have a chance, I'm going to report you. You will be executed immediately," exclaimed Decker.

"You are right Kolonel. I guess I have to do something about it," said Jennifer picking up a fluffy pillow from the floor. She placed it over Kolonel Decker face and held it there. Decker struggled as best as he could in his weakened state. He even broke free and shouted for his aide but only for a second before Jennifer was back on top of him with the pillow firmly over his nose and mouth. The Kolonel quickly stopped jerking around and he laid still.

There was a knock on the bedroom door with the Kolonel's aide calling for him. Jennifer got up and cracked the door. "Ya?" she asked calmly.

"Kolonel me call," said the aide in a lame attempt to speak English.

Jennifer just looked at him smiled and shook her head before easing the door shut in the aide's face. She returned to the Kolonel. He was dead as fried pork. It was going to be a long night for the American girl, having to sack out on the floor with a dead man in the room.

¥

Captain Jennifer Edwards of the American Army Corp succumbed to her illness three weeks later. One night she went to sleep and did not wake up. The new camp Kommandant sort of honored Kolonel Decker's request and treated her with respect. He was somewhat surprised when Jennifer slept with him and they had relations. Even though Jennifer's letters to Colonel Daniels were butchered by the German censors, the Bomber Girl's life in the camp was well documented. Captain Edwards was credited with killing 14 German Generals, many who were handpicked by Hitler himself: 22 Colonels and an assorted number of Majors and Captains. In addition, Captain Edwards flew 17 bombing missions before being shot down.

One day a uniformed man came to Jennifer's South Carolina home. He regretted to inform her parents that Jennifer died in the line of duty. He then proceeded to present the couple with a Distinguished Service Cross for her selfless sacrifice for her nation. The man left leaving Jennifer's parents with more question than answers. If they were alive today, they would have their answers. Sometimes, the worst thing about being a parent is not being able to tell your children how proud you are of them.

¥

Many B-25s of the 10th were shot down. The surviving crews were of course captured. Many were raped giving the American Bomber Girls their chance to complete their mission. The German doctors were at a loss as to why perfectly healthy young German women on the home front were dying from simple ailments such as a cold or flu. The German doctors were also at a loss as to why whole barracks of young, seemingly healthy German troops died after becoming sick. The virus created a strain on the already over extended medical system.

None of the 10th survived the war. If anti-aircraft batteries didn't kill them, their own personal illness did. As the war progressed, the need for female aviators lessened. The 10th and 366th losses were not replaced leading to the flights being disbanded at the end of 1944.

CHAPTER 36

LIEUTENANT VIRGINIA WHITE

"Captain to crew, we are going down! I'll hold her steady, everyone bail out, bail out!!" said Jennifer calmly into the intercom, "You too Honey. I'll try and hold her steady."

Virginia donned her parachute and dropped out of the hatch in the bomb bay following Marie. The lieutenant was scared half out of her mind but once she was floating toward the Earth, she calmed down and enjoyed the view. She saw 'The Albatross' left engine belching smoke as it lost altitude.

Virginia could see a stand of pines quickly approaching. Instinctively, she pulled and tugged on the parachute lines attempting to veer off to the right. She had a reasonably soft landing in a field narrowly missing the trees. After unbuckling her harness, the girl dashed for the pines to get out of sight.

Once in the trees, the American girl could hear moaning and coughing. She quickly pulled her .45 from its holster and followed the sounds. Virginia was horrified to find Teresa who could not avoid drifting into a large old pine. Virginia found her with a broken bough driven through her chest. There was nothing Virginia could do for her friend. Teresa was dead. Lieutenant Teresa Gallo passed after bailing out of the wounded war bird.

"Oh Teresa," said Virginia aloud.

Virginia holstered her gun and started to trek south. She was nervous and a little scared but kept her head while cautiously slipping through the thick under brush but before too long, she was surrounded by a patrol of German soldiers. The first thought she had was to run, but after a moment common sense prevailed so she surrendered. Her second thought was the mission to 'kill Krauts' as they dubbed their task.

Virginia froze. The Germans stared at the American girl and said a few things amongst themselves. After a few brief moments, two young German soldiers, who didn't say anything, began to push and shove the petit girl between themselves. One took Virginia's .45 and then threw her to the ground. Once in the dirt and dry leaves another soldier kicked her in the ribs and once in the abdomen. She had the wind knocked out of her but being a tough little girl, she managed to get back to her feet only to receive a back hand across the chops and down she went again. She was lying on her back when all the Germans began brutally tearing at Virginia's uniform.

"Easy guys," she implored, "why so rough?"

A German slapped the girl in the face and doled out another blow to her stomach. She saw stars and gasped for a breath. Virginia put up her hands but only to stop the brutal attack. The Germans viewed that action as resistance and the little girl received yet another slap across the face. She laid on her stomach pulling her knees under her body. A German turned Virginia on her back and proceeded to lift her legs and pull her shoes from her feet tossing them aside while another unbuckled her belt and tore open her pants before pulling them completely off. Virginia protested only to receive another slap to the face. A soldier fumbled with Virginia's leather jacket. Another ripped open her shirt scattering the buttons across the forest floor before removing it and then removed her brassiere with his knife. She was more than a little frightened by the assailants' savagery. The Germans stripped the American girl down to just her underwear.

When the Germans were done, Virginia laid motionless in the dirt gasping for breath as she watched the first soldier undo his pants. Just as the soldier took two handfuls of Virginia's underwear, there was a big ado amongst the other soldiers. An officer had pulled up in a German style JEEP just appalled by what his men were doing to the American flyer and angered by their behavior. Virginia could hear the officer yelling at the other men. She could see them hang their heads and fall into formation and then march off.

Virginia sat up with her arms folded across her bare chest. The officer gathered up her clothing and kneeled down to help the American dress, holding her shirt open for Virginia to glide her arm into the sleeve. "I'm sorry for the ill behavior of my troops, young lady," said the officer in fine English. "They are young and feel they have the right to mistreat an American female flyer." The officer helped Virginia with her pants and shirt. Her bra was a total loss.

"I suppose you are expecting a big thank you, aren't you Fritz?" said Virginia. "I had everything under control…I didn't need your help."

The officer ignored Virginia and continued to assist the American dress actually collecting her shoes and putting them back on her feet. "Are you hurt? Oh damn, your lip is bleeding," he said taking a handkerchief from his pocket and wiping the corner of Virginia's mouth.

"I'll be fine," said Virginia, pushing his hand away. "You speak English well Fritz. Where did you learn?"

"Catholic Seminary in Oregon. I was going to be a priest until I met my wife…after that, all my plans drastically changed. How about you? You don't look old enough to be a flyer. How old are you?"

"Don't tell anyone but I'm 17."

"The Americans are drafting people that young? Things must be pretty bad in the states."

"No, you have it all wrong, Fritz. I wanted to enlist so I forged my paperwork."

"Why do you keep calling me Fritz?"

"No offence…we call all the Germans Fritz."

"I'm not offended…that's my name. Captain Fritz Augustus at your service. Ahhh, what's your name?"

Virginia sorta chuckled, "Lieutenant Virginia White U.S. Army Air Force."

"Well Lieutenant, if you would be so good to step into my car, I'll drive you to your new home. Please don't try running away."

"Where do you think I'm going to run to, Captain? Give me a moment to adjust my uniform"

Captain Augustus sat in his rig patiently waiting for Virginia to try and close up her shirt tucking it into her pants then tying her shoe laces. "You ahhhh about ready there ahhh Lieutenant? The war is going to be over soon."

"Ok, I'm ready," said Virginia scampering up into the car.

The German started down a dirt road that emptied onto a two lane paved highway in the country. "You know you could just drop me off at the Swiss border," said Virginia.

"Ya und I can get life in front of the firing squad," replied Fritz.

"You have a family?" asked Virginia.

"Ya, a boy Peter who is eight and a girl Petre who is six, and my wife of course."

The two did not have much to say after that. Fritz asked how she became a flyer but Virginia did not want to talk about that for fear of saying something about the mission. "The ride to the camp is not long," announced the Captain. "It won't be so bad. There is a group of captured Russian women there. You will be kept with them separate from the men of course."

Fritz pulled his car into the front gate and up to the Kommandant's office. Two soldiers approached the car, saluted the Captain and then opened the door for Virginia. "Just obey the rules, Virginia and you will be fine. I'll look in on you from time to time."

"Whatever you say Fritz," said Virginia with a snarl in her voice, then she watched the Captain drive off leaving her behind.

After a short meeting with the Kommandant, Virginia was shown to her barracks. Few prison camps in Germany housed Russian women prisoners. The women were usually captured civilians or Jews or brave Russian girls who operated a machine gun nest. Some were snipers or they picked up a gun from a fallen soldier and started shooting. They were kept in a separate fenced in area with their own barracks.

CHAPTER 37

VIRGINIA'S PRISON TIME

Just like any prison, time passes slowly in a POW camp even for women. Virginia became accustomed to her fate behind the wire resigning herself that she was probably going to die there due to her illness. She opted not to mention it to anyone for fear of risking 'The Mission'. So she spent her time learning Russian so she could speak with the women around her. She met a young Jewish girl named Lila. Lila was only a couple of years older than her. They became fast friends despite the language barrier. Russian is a hard language to learn. They have many sounds that English does not have. Even so, Virginia picked up the language quickly but was only able to speak of simple ideas. When issues became too complex, the conversation only ended in frustration.

The women would sew, do tats and knit. One girl would find scraps of cloth and make quilts, a talent she learned from her mother and went on to teach to the others. The Red Cross gave them musical instruments and a few started an orchestra. They became quite good. Then there were singing groups who formed and a choir that put on a show once a week.

After a few weeks, Fritz fulfilled his promise and stopped in to check up on Virginia. After briefly speaking to the Kommandant, Virginia saw him crossing the compound toward the women's lock up area. He had a good sized package with him. When he arrived at the gate, a German soldier beckoned Virginia. "Hello, Virginia," said Fritz, "told you I'd be back."

Virginia stepped out into the yard with Fritz, the first time she was out of her confines. "Hello Fritz," said Virginia with a small smile. "What's in the package?"

"Here, open it."

"You know I'm not allowed to accept…. IT'S A NEW OFFICER'S DRESS UNIFORM!!!" she shouted. "How did you do it?"

"I'm still affiliated with the Catholic Church and we work closely with the Red Cross. I explained it was my fault you have to wear rags, so well you can figure out the rest. My wife is a fairly good seamstress. We used a girl in our town that is built like you and tailored the uniform for you. We shortened the pants and sleeves, took in the waist and had to take some out of the seat. I hope it fits."

"I'm putting it on…I'll use the officers' latrine, after all, I am a Lieutenant."

Virginia slipped into the men's room and quickly stripped off her old and torn uniform. She was standing in just her underwear when a soldier came in. She just smiled at him before neatly opening the papered bundle and laying out the new clothes. The German smiled back and did his business ever watching the young naked American girl dress, and then he left.

Included in the package, Virginia found some simple make-up that Fritz's wife slipped in. Before she put on the Eisenhower cut jacket, Virginia did her eyes with mascara, her lips in some lipstick and powdered on some foundation followed by a hint of rouge. She kept her lieutenant bars and other insignias from the old outfit.

Fritz patiently waited outside for the girl, talking to the guards about nothing of importance. Finally the unveiling. There were ohhhs and ahhhs and a few whistles from the Germans when Virginia stepped out of the bathroom. Rightfully so, because even though she was barely a teenager, Virginia was a beautiful lady.

"You look….really, really nice," said Fritz.

"Thanks," said Virginia smiling. "And tell your wife thank you for the gift. Am I allowed to accept a gift from you?"

"It is common for the Red Cross to send replacement uniforms so you're ok."

"I'll keep my ragged uniform for common day and wear this one on special occasions."

"You have special occasions in a POW camp?" asked Fritz.

"Sure we do. We are having a dance here tomorrow night. Would you like to be my date?"

"The only man in a room full of Russian women prisoners? I'd rather go to the Western front." They both laughed.

The duo strolled the compound unmolested by guards. Virginia spoke of life in the prison while Fritz told her about his family. "Fritz, will you keep a secret?" asked Virginia.

"That's my job Virginia."

"Promise?"

"Sure."

"Some of the girls trade sexual favors with the guards. I hear that if a prisoner gets pregnant, she will be executed. Is that true?"

"Only the women prisoners," said Fritz. "If the men get pregnant we let that go."

"Be serious," said Virginia with a laugh.

"Ok, Virginia. Don't do it. If you become pregnant, you will be shot. And the German soldier will be shot as well."

"Huh, then it is true," said Virginia.

They walked along in silence. Telling Fritz about her life in a prison only took a moment. It was time for Fritz to go back to the war. Virginia gathered up her old uniform and other things from Fritz's package and headed back toward her barracks. When she got there, Virginia shared the make-up with any of the women who were interested…it wasn't meant to last.

¥

Two months passed. Captain Fritz was good about making frequent visits bringing the American girl gifts. Fritz was 20 years older than Virginia and sort of adopted her as the daughter he never had. "But you have a daughter," Virginia pointed out.

"Yes, but you are the daughter I never had," said Fritz.

One day while they were strolling the compound, Captain Fritz asked Virginia some things that were on his mind for a while.

"You never told me how you became a flyer," said Fritz.

"Not much to tell, Fritz, I was in the Army and they were looking for smart women with small stature to fly the B-25s and bomb the crap out of the German industries. I applied and was chosen."

"How many missions did you fly?" Virginia did not answer. "I don't think you would be divulging vital military secrets about how many missions you flew."

"Fritz, what does it mater? I don't want to talk about it, I'm stuck here lessen you want to drive me to Switzerland."

"I'm sorry Virginia. I won't bring it up anymore."

They walked quietly for a while. "The wife would like to have you over for dinner one night."

"See if you can get me a 24 hour pass," said Virginia, chuckling.

They did not have much more to talk about and Fritz had to leave but he promised to be back.

That night, while everyone was asleep in the barracks, the door of Virginia's hut sprang open and three guards burst in. They pulled Virginia from her bed and dragged her outside. It was a cool night and all Virginia wore was her t-shirt and underwear. She was a little frightened because she thought she was going to be shot.

The guards led the American girl to the rec hall. Inside, she was confronted by two other guards, the Kommandant, and three big men dressed in traditional black Gestapo uniforms. "Is this the flyer?" demand a Gestapo man.

"Ya," answered the Kommandant. He appeared to be frightened.

"I am Major Strasser. All you have to do, little girl, is answer a few simple questions and you will be retuned to your bed. How long have you been a flyer?"

Virginia stood quietly with her arms folded across her chest. She was more than a little intimidated by the large black clad man who was three times her size and twice her weight.

"Tell use what we want to know," continued the Gestapo agent.

"VVVVVirginia WWWWWhite," she whispered, "Lieutenant, 15316101."

"No girl you are not going to get away with that. Tell me, why are you a flyer? What is your mission?"

'My mission,' thought Virginia, *'To kill Krauts. Does he know something?'* "Virginia White, Lieutenant, 475389210."

"Ya, I heard that tell me something new."

"Virginia Whi....."

She was cut short by a slap across the face. "What is your mission Virginia White?" The American girl was silently rubbing her face. "Ok we will start with something simple. Where is your base? Who is your commanding officer?" Virginia didn't say anything. She received another slap from the other Gestapo man.

Virginia fell to the floor. She rose to all fours only to receive the toe of a boot to the gut. The girl fell on the floor again this time curled up in a ball gasping for breath. The German then kicked her once more in the middle of the back then he dropped down on one knee. The Major sprawled Virginia on her back, balled up her t-shirt in his fist and pulled her head off the floor.

"Are you ready to tell me what I want to know?"

"I don't know what you want!!" Virginia lied.

"Yes, I think you do," said the Major before back handing the girl again. "Strip her," he ordered the guards. The guards were reluctant to follow the Major's order because Virginia was one of their prisoners and they were not permitted to mistreat the prisoners without cause. "You heard me," said Strasser, "take her shirt off."

They dragged Virginia to her feet and then ripped her t-shirt from her body. Virginia pulled away from them and struggled. "Go ahead hit me again you Gestapo pig…I'm starting to like it"

Sure enough, the other Gestapo officer cold cocked Virginia in the side of the head. She dropped to the floor unconscious. "You knocked her out you fool. Someone find a bucket of water," shouted Strasser. It took a little time but a guard brought a bucket of ice cold water. The Major doused the sleeping girl in the face with it.

Virginia woke gagging and spitting. The water went up her nose. "You still here?" she said when she was fully awake. "You should go."

"Tie her hands," said the Major.

Virginia's hands were bound together by rope and then the other end of the rope was tossed over the rafter of the ceiling joists. They pulled on the end of the rope standing the nude American girl on her toes and then tied-off the rope. She hung there helpless cold and shivering in front of all those Germans.

The Major pinched Virginia's chin and mouth in his black gloved hand. "We will start again. What is your mission?"

Virginia got her knee up and into the groin of the Major. He fell back but stayed on his feet groaning in pain. He was shocked by the girl's pluck. "I'm done playing with you Virginia White." The Major took his knife from its sheath on his belt and stepped behind Virginia. He then sliced the girl's skin just below her left breast.

Virginia moaned but not very loud only to have her skin under her right breast also sliced. Blood flowed from the wounds and dripped on the floor. The Major wrapped an arm around Virginia's body and brought his knife across her stomach. Virginia did not scream or yell but deeply quietly groaned. The cuts were not deep and did not do any serious damage but cuts such as those really hurt. Tears began to run down the young American Bomber Girls face. The Gestapo major appeared irritated that Virginia just murmured and did not scream in pain.

"Now tell me, what is your mission?"

"I'm a navigator on a B-25 Mitchell bomber. My missions are to bomb the stuffing out of German factories. To date I have flown eleven missions. I killed your mutter and your grandmutter"

Major Stauser sliced her side, "Is that all?"

Virginia groaned in pain, "ISN'T THAT ENOUGH!!??" she cried out.

The Major sliced her leg for her insolence. "Where is your base?"

The American blustered again. "Har…Har," Virginia was about to divulge the all-girl air base but her second wind breezed in. "Berlin. You miserable pig."

Strauser lost his composure and backhanded the American girl on the side of the head knocking her into three weeks. Her unconscious body hung by the arms while the cords dug deep into her wrists. "Get some more water," ordered Stauser. A sergeant splashed the whole bucket of ice cold water into Virginia's face.

"YOU MISERABLE PIG," shouted the girl when she woke.

The Major had had enough of this girl. He stepped behind the girl and pulled her head back by the hair exposing the muscles in her throat. He was about to use the knife for the last time when the door of the rec hall suddenly opened. In stepped Captain Fritz. He had charged one of the guards with looking after Virginia and to phone him if she was in trouble…and this was trouble.

"Major Strasser, stop this now!" Fritz ordered.

"Lord Augustus, why are you here?"

'Lord Augustus,' thought Virginia to herself.

"I was about to ask you the same question," said Fritz taking a blanket from a shelf and wrapping Virginia in it. Then he unsheathed his own knife and cut the ropes suspending the American girl. She collapsed in his arms and he gently laid her on the blood soaked floor.

"There has been an outbreak of deaths due to simple illnesses in the vicinity. Our doctors have found a strange unknown virus in the blood of all the dead. The virus is ONLY found in areas where American female flyers are held captive. Our contacts in England confirmed that the Americans are doing something but they don't know what. I believe that girl you are protecting knows something and we need to find out. She was ready to crack before you interrupted me. I will finish my interrogation and get the truth from her."

"This interrogation is over. You have done enough damage to this poor young girl. If she hasn't told you anything useful by now she has nothing to tell you."

"Lord Augustus, this girl knows something, I can tell."

"You are done here Strasser. Now get out or I'll have you shot!!"

Major Strasser knew when he was beat so he and his men slinked from the rec room, loaded into their Mercedes and drove away. Fritz then turned his attention back to Virginia still wrapped in the blanket but sitting up on the floor with her head hung in front of her. She had lost too much blood and with her illness, she could die without warning. Captain Augustus scooped Virginia up into his arms and took her outside and set her on the passenger seat of his car.

"What are you doing?" demanded the Kommandant.

"I'm taking her to the hospital in town. She needs medical help, more than you can provide." The Captain roared out of the gate. He was jamming gears making all due speed on the paved highway toward town.

Virginia had passed out in the rec room but the cold air woke her up. "You bastard," she said.

"What did you say?" asked Fritz.

"You heard me, you bastard. Stop the car!! Stop the car right now or I'll jump out while it's moving!!!"

Fritz slammed on the brakes almost flinging the girl through the front windshield. Virginia stepped out of the car and started walking down the road wearing only her underwear and a blanket wrapped around her.

"What are you doing!?" yelled Fritz.

"I'm walking to Switzerland Lord Augustus! If you want to stop me you will have to shoot me."

"Virginia, you are not thinking clearly. Get back in the car," said Fritz following Virginia.

"NO!"

"Ok, go to Switzerland without clothes or shoes. But will you please tell me why you are so upset."

"Why am I upset?? You don't know that I know you sicked the Gestapo on me!"

"Why do you think that?"

Virginia turned around to face Fritz. "Oh, it's just coincidence that the Gestapo shows up on the same day you do and asking the same questions as you did."

"Yes it is, Virginia"

"You are so full of crap Loooord Augustussss. You must have met some pretty dumb girls living in Orrrr-a-goooon but us Ohio girls are much smarter." Virginia turned and started to walk down the road, and then she turned again and returned to the car. "And another thing, we have German POW camps in the United States. In the south, the Germans work in the fields picking cotton. On weekends, we give them money and allow them to go to town to see a movie or go out to dinner or meet a nice American girl. German POW's have more and better rights than our colored people. We don't carve them up like a Thanksgiving Day turkey!" She turned again and walked down the road.

"Go ahead, walk to Switzerland you stubborn silly American girl. See if I give a damn!!" Fritz climbed back into his Jeep and watched Virginia walk away in the vehicle's partially blackened head lights. He did not have to wait long before Virginia collapsed to the pavement.

When Fritz walked to her side, he found the girl lying flat on her back with the blanket laid open. For the first time he could see the slits the Major had made with his knife. Once again he wrapped the petite girl in the blanket. It was soaked in blood to the point of dripping onto the road and running down Captain Fritz's uniform. He put her in the passenger seat of his car. "How the hell did you stay on your feet this long?" he said aloud.

CHAPTER 38

VIRGINIA RECIEVES A 24 HOUR PASS

Virginia was flying. She was soaring through the clouds high over the German landscape sans a plane, wings or a propeller. Deutschland from way up there was a beautiful country with hills, forests, and old ruins of once great castles. The countryside was dotted with farms and vineyards. From her bird's eye view, there were no bombed out cities, or front lines, or rear echelons just old farm houses. That's when the American girl woke up.

It was only a dream, but a truly vivid one at that. One of those visions we all have in the early morn just before the alarm clock starts screaming. A dream so real we can reach out and touch it or we recall the images during the day.

Virginia woke to find herself in a very comfortable hospital bed with her head on a fluffy down pillow. She had absolutely no clue where she was. Her hopes of being in England were quickly dashed when a pretty young nurse entered her room and began speaking in her tongue. A dead giveaway that Virginia was still in Germany.

After a moment or two, the fog between her ears lifted. The last thing she remembered was being on the road to town with Captain Fritz. *'That lying traitor,'* she thought in her head even though she could not recall what he did to betray her. Then she recollected the Gestapo Major slicing her up…she shivered.

Virginia gingerly lifted the blankets and saw that she was neatly wrapped in bandages around the torso. The only thing she was clad in was a new pair of underwear. "I must be the most naked officer in the whole damn war," she said to herself. She quickly checked her arms. Colonel Daniels had mentioned that if the Germans took blood for testing, she would find a purple dot on the inside of the elbow. There was none. The nurse had gone and brought back an older woman who, just like American nurses, she immediately began poking and prodding Virginia. The old nurse checked Virginia's pulse, blood pressure and temperature. It was a little high.

Being a bright girl, Virginia had picked-up on some of the German language. Outside of a few sounds that English does not have, the two languages are not that different. Virginia was left alone in her room with the exception of the old nurse prodding her once in a while and the young nurse who brought her meals. The American girl tried to talk with the young German nurse but that proved to be futile mostly because the nurse refused to cooperate with the American. Virginia stayed in bed for the remainder of the first day and until noon the next day when she struggled to her feet. She just had to stretch. The German nurses had still not given her anything to wear when the doctor came to her room accompanied by Captain Fritz. Virginia was standing at the window in just her underwear watching the street below. She did not cover up but put her hands on her waist. "Don't you people know how to knock?" she demanded sternly.

The Captain and Doctor look at each other while Virginia covered up with a blanket. Fritz said something to the doctor who quickly left the room.

"How are you, Lieutenant?" asked Fritz. "The doctor is going to fetch you some PJ's."

"PJ's, that's funny. It's not something you would expect a German to say," said Virginia chuckling. "I'm fine. I would normally ask 'When can I go home?' but that question seems moot these days. What's happening in the world? Are we still at war?"

"Yes…afraid so, Virginia."

"Who's winning?"

"No one," said Fritz. "You have been asleep for four days. How do you feel?"

"Alright. I'm still mad at you! Do you mind reminding my why?"

"You thought I called the Gestapo Major to torture you."

"Oh yeah. Well…did you?"

"No Virginia, that is just not my way. Here, I brought you your uniform from the POW camp. The doctor wants to examine your cuts. Then after you get dressed, I got you a 24 hour pass to be my guest at my house for dinner tonight."

"Gee, swell," said Virginia sarcastically.

Captain Fritz went to the hospital office to use the phone while the doctor changed Virginia's bandages. He was pleased with how well the tough American girl was healing. The cuts were not deep but some needed a few extra sutures. Virginia showered and dressed. Being low maintenance, she was ready in about half an hour. Fritz escorted her outside. There were people passing her on the sidewalk on the way to Fritz's car but they did not seem to give the American girl a second glance.

"You would think that these people see an American Army officer on the street every day," observed Virginia.

"You're with me so I guess they are not concerned," said Fritz.

Virginia hopped into Fritz's car to make the journey out of town to Fritz's house down a two lane paved road. "I see you cleaned up all my blood," she said. "Don't you want to drill me about my flying career some more?" Virginia asked with a hint of malice.

"Look Virginia, I said I was sorry about all that and I would not bring it up again! Now do you want to argue or have a nice evening away from the world's troubles?"

"Ok ok, I won't mention it again." There was a brief moment of silence. "What's your wife like?"

"She is a sweet, warm, friendly beautiful lady. You two have much in common. I think you will like her. She is dying to meet you."

"One should be careful of dying for anything these days…you just might get it!" said Virginia.

After a half hour drive, the duo arrived at Fritz's home. Well, it was what he called home…It was a big, beautiful sprawling villa on an estate the size of an Ohio county just outside of the small German town. Fritz brought the car around to the front door.

"This is your house!?" said Virginia

"Yes it is. It has been in the family for nearly 500 years."

"What are you royalty or something?"

"Ahhhh, yes," said Fritz. They walked up to the door. "Now my wife is different from most German ladies so if you would please not say anything about it when you meet her," said Fritz as they went inside.

"Of course Fritz. What kind of insensitive boob do you take me for."

"Hello, I'm Lady Augustus," said Fritz wife upon meeting Virginia.

"YOU'RE COLORED!!" announced Virginia. Fritz slapped the side of his face and shook his head.

"I am!?? Fritz, you should have told me!" said Lady Augustus smiling. "Linda Savage, at your service. I'm from Oregon."

"Linda, allow me to present Lieutenant Virginia White," said the Captain.

"Pleased to meet you, Miss White. Fritz has told me alot about you."

"Please, call me Gini. Nice to meet you too Linda. Fritz has told me nothing about you," said Virginia giving the Captain a nasty glance.

"Well c'mon in and met the family," said Linda. "My son Peter, he's eight and my little angel Petre, she's six."

"Are you really an American flyer?" asked Peter. A big kid for eight with black curly hair and mocha skin.

"Peter," scolded Fritz.

"It's ok Fritz. Yes Peter, I am."

"What kind of plane do you fly on?"

"A Mitchell B-25 bomber."

"Did you even shoot down any planes?"

"No, I'm a navigator. I make sure the plane gets to where it is going then home again. Except for my last flight we didn't quite get back home."

"Peter, no more questions. Run along you can talk with the Lieutenant at dinner. I'm sorry again, Virginia."

"That's ok Fritz. Boys are inquisitive no matter what side of the pond they are on."

Dinner was served and uneventful. Peter wanted to talk about airplanes with the American lieutenant while Petre, a cute little princess with lighter skin, blue eyes and blonde straight hair, sat quietly and listened. Periodically she would speak with her mother in German. The children learned English from their mother since their birth. Linda's cook made Sauer braten. If some one has never had a properly cooked Sauer braten, they are really missing out. Linda wished she could make cheeseburgers and French fries in honor of her guest.

After dinner, the Captain stoked a blaze in the large open hearth in the really huge living room. He then went to put the children to bed leaving the ladies alone with their German beers sitting in front of the fire.

"You guys been married long?" asked Virginia.

"Eight years," answered Linda with a smile.

"Ahh Linda, you have an eight year old…you wanna elaborate on that."

"I met Fritz while he was in seminary in St. Benedict, Oregon way before the war. It was not unusual for Germans wanting to be priests to do their school work there. I was working as a waitress in a diner and Fritz and his friends would come in for dinner every Friday and Saturday night. I understand the food at the abbey was not very good," she said with a smile.

Linda had a pretty smile that created a pair of dimples in each corner of her mouth suspended by her distinct high cheek bones and dark eyes. Virginia deduced that Linda had some American Indian blood also because she was not dark but had more caramel colored skin and straight jet black hair.

"I went to the St. Benedict abbey with my Baptist church for a picnic one Sunday and finally had an opportunity to be alone with Fritz and to get to know him. We ended up missing the whole event because we spent the day behind the church. We didn't do nothin', just shot the shit," she giggled and then so did Virginia.

"And then, two weeks later," continued Linda, "I went on a rafting trip. It had nothing to do with the town or the church or work; it was just a rafting trip with some friends. Well, you never guess who showed up."

"The big bad Kraut," said Virginia.

"You got it. We just have like interests. So any how, the group of rafts took a break down stream. Again Fritz and I strolled away from the crowd and were alone. Gini, it was love at first sight and there was nothing any body could do about it and neither could we."

"You're shitting me right?"

"Are not! His collar came off, then my clothes and then I found out about Peter two months later."

"That, that pretty much sealed that deal."

"Afraid so. I came back to Germany with Fritz. His dreams of being a priest were over but he serves the All Mighty in many ways still." They laughed together and then were silent for a moment.

"You could have done worse, Linda," said Virginia.

"I have baby, I have." They laughed together again.

"Don't you miss the States?'

"Not too much. Here in Germany, there are no colored people. No bigotry or hatred toward my people. Life is easier for this little nigger girl." Again they were quiet.

"You know Gini I heard about your little run in with the Gestapo. Fritz and I talk and he tells me everything secret or not. He admires you and had nothing to do with the Gestapo major interrogating you. He is a good man and feels bad about it. Ya know?"

"Yeah I am starting to believe it."

"It's true, Gini."

Virginia drew a deep sigh, "Whatever you say Linda, you never lied to me before."

Fritz finally joined the ladies once Petre was asleep. "Here you go Virginia I brought you a fresh beer."

"Thanks Captain, come sit next to me so I can steal you away from Linda."

"No thanks, I don't date 13 year olds!!"

They all laughed, "I'm 17 almost 18," said Virginia in her defense. They all laughed and had a nice evening.

They sat by the fire and talked past midnight. Virginia stayed the night. She had her own room…her own room was the size of her whole house in Ohio…a minute exaggeration…the room had its own zip code. The next morning, after a nice German breakfast, she and Fritz had to return to the war.

CHAPTER 39

VIRGINIA SAVES A LIFE

Being a prisoner of war means never being able to make decisions for one self. Much like being in any military but as a prisoner, to disobey an order could get oneself shot. Even though Virginia had a friend who was very influential, she still had to behave well and toe the line.

Captain Fitz arranged for Virginia to stay in the hospital until the stitches needed to be removed. Fritz and Linda had a full agenda the day after the dinner so she remained in her room with three other girls. It was not so bad. The German girls made an effort to talk with her and were even friendly with the American girl. They played a German card game called 'Skat' (pronounced Scott). Virginia tried to teach them 'Go Fish'. It was complicated with her limited Deutsch… 'Fische Gehen.' It loses something in the translation.

The following day Linda left the children with the sitter, came to the hospital and signed Virginia out. "I have a special day planned for us," said Linda. "Something I have always wanted to do for a while but never took the time."

"I don't care what it is as long as it's far away from here," said Virginia.

The two Americans drove off in Linda's 1940 Mercedes Benz. It was the finest car Virginia had ever ridden in. After some small talk, she asked where they were going. "There is a brewery on the edge of town," explained Linda with a smile. "I just haven't found time to go until now. We are going to go on a tour through the brewery and then we get to sample their wares at the end."

"Does it matter that I'm 17 years old?"

"You're in Germany now girl! They don't care how old you are. Besides, in that uniform you look alot older."

They arrived at the brewery, went inside and queued up with the other visitors. Again, in this small town away from all the shelling and bombing at the front, most of the people graciously accepted the two obvious Americans as guests instead of enemies. There were a few mean glares all the same.

The tour was interesting, fun and informative. Neither woman had ever been inside a brewery before. The tour guide explained things and Linda quietly translated most of it to Virginia. Virginia, of course, had to make her little quips throughout the tour. At the end of the tour, they were privy to mugs of the house beers along with wurst and brotchen (much like an American roll). Linda became a little…alot tipsy and they walked around the pond outside the brewery before driving home.

On the ride home, they joked about the trip, the kids and Captain Fritz. They were both happy and not feeling any pain. Linda drove damn good being three sheets to the wind. She dropped Virginia off at the hospital. "I'm kinda busy tomorrow, Virginia…but the next day we will do something I promise. I trust you are going inside and not running to Switzerland?" asked Linda.

"Naaaa," said Virginia, "running to Switzerland would take effort. I ain't got none of that! Whatcha doin' tomorrow?" asked Virginia.

"I'm doing a fundraiser for the soldiers at the front. Some ladies are coming to the house tomorrow after lunch. It's the kind of thing us royalty have to do. I doubt you would want to attend."

"What…an American Bomber Girl collecting monies for the German war effort. Why would I miss that? I'll wear my best uniform, actually my only uniform."

"I'll see you in a couple of days, Virginia," said Linda laughing at the girl's antics. "I've had a good time."

"Me too," said Virginia. "Thank you and I'll see you." She waved bye as Linda drove away, then returned to her room.

¥

Nighttime in the German hospital is usually quiet. Unlike in the US, the nurses in a German hospital don't barge in every five minutes throwing on the lights wanting to poke and prod at the patents. Unlike in the US, patents in German hospitals actually get some sleep.

While Virginia and Linda were enjoying their tour of the brewery, the young girl in the bed next to Virginia was in surgery having her appendix removed. She was resting comfortably until about three in the morning when Virginia was awakened by her coughing. When the fog in her brain cleared, Virginia realized the girl was choking to death. Virginia jumped from her bed and rushed to the girl's bedside. Putting her fist under the girl's neck, Virginia pulled her head back to clear the German girls passage way, pinched her nose and then blew into the girl's mouth attempting to put air into her lungs. It was to no avail. The girl's throat was sealed tight and she was not getting any air. By that time the other two girls were at her side, Virginia quickly turned on the lights and found a tray with some medical instruments on it. She found a scalpel and some plastic tubing used for IV's.

"Hold her down!" Virginia shouted to the other bewildered German girls. "Hold...her...down," said Virginia holding both the choking girl's arms tight to her side. The girl understood. "You hold her head," said Virginia to her other room mate.

With the choking girl restrained, the American found the base of her throat. She carefully made an incision with the scalpel severing the choking girl's larynx. Blood began to flow, the girl's body jerked and she loudly moaned. Virginia's helpers look a bit faint but held the choking girl down.

Virginia tried to force the tube into the girl's larynx but it was too big. "Damn," she said. She gently used the scalpel to scrape the larynx to make it larger and trimmed the tubing to make it thinner while blood squirted in her face and on the bed. Virginia was successful and the tube slid easily into the larynx. She blew air into the tube and into the choking girl's lungs. The girl suck the air in then expelled it on her own but Virginia blew air in a second and third time to be sure she was breathing on her own.

The girls all began to relax until the door of their room opened and big orderly busted in. All he saw was a smiling American girl hovering over a German girl with her throat sliced open. The large German cold-cocked Virginia in the side of her head. The much smaller exhausted American girl instantly saw stars. She folded like a house of cards crumbling to the floor.

The orderly filled his hands with Virginia's hospital gown, lifted the unconscious girl from the floor and flopped her down on her bed like a rag doll. He then retrieved some restraints and tied Virginia's wrists and ankles to the bed frame. He left her there not bothering to cover her with a blanket on the cool night. Not that it mattered; Virginia was out like a light.

¥

It was past noon when Virginia woke the next day to see Captain Augustus through the slits of her eyes. He was sitting on a chair next to her bed with a cold bag of ice pressed against her bruised head. She was covered with a blanket and the bindings were gone. "Fritz," she murmured, "what are you doing here? Where are we? What happened? Why does my head hurt?"

"What's the last thing you remember?" asked the Captain.

"Being slammed in the side of the head with a pile driver. No…the girl, SHE'S DYING!" said Virginia sitting up quickly. "Ow, ow, ow my head."

The Captain slowly and gently laid Virginia back on her pillow. "She's fine thanks to you. She is recovering from your surgery. You know in our country, you need a license to do what you did."

"What happened to her?"

"It appears that the girl had an allergic reaction to the antibiotics the hospital gave her. Her throat clamped shut tight as a fist. Where did you learn how to do a tracheotomy?"

"The USAAF thinks that the navigator doesn't have enough to do what with all the math and watching the maps...so we had to take an advanced life saving course and be the medic on the plane."

"Well, you saved that girl's life. The doctor said that two minutes more and she would have died. The hospital is all a buzz with the story. They are going to bake you a cake and all bring it up here."

"Let me guess...a German chocolate cake."

The Captain chuckled, "Actually, yes it is."

"Entschuldigen Sie, bitte," (pardon me, please) said the big German orderly who decked Virginia the night before.

"This is the orderly who belted you. He has something to say," said Fritz.

The big man spoke and Fritz translated. The orderly profusely apologized for hitting Virginia in the head. He wanted to make up for it and asked if there was ANYTHING at all she wanted.

"Yeah, to go home!" said Virginia.

Fritz drew a heavy sigh. "Anything else Virginia?" he asked.

"How about a cheeseburger and fries?" The big German did not understand 'cheese burger'. "And chocolate ice cream," added Virginia.

"Ah so," he said before leaving the room.

"He understood that?" asked Virginia.

"Ya," said Fritz. "It sounds the same in German."

"Ok. He didn't have to apologize...I would have never known it was him who hit me."

"He wanted to. He feels really bad."

There was a quiet period in which neither one spoke but Virginia laid in bed with the ice pack on her check.

The silence was broken by a Major entering the room, "Achtung," said the Major.

Fritz came to attention while Virginia just opened her eyes. The Major was accompanied by a General followed by half the hospital staff. Fritz and the General spoke before the Captain turned to Virginia.

"Am I in trouble?" asked Virginia.

" Naaa, the General wishes to talk with you. Can you sit up?"

"Can you help me?"

Fritz assisted Virginia up so she sat on the edge of the bed with the blanket around her. The General snapped off a salute to Virginia who returned a salute back. The General spoke as Fritz translated. He said something about these times heroes are heroes blinded by the nationalities and uniform. On behalf of all the German people everywhere, he wished to award the American girl the Iron Cross Fourth Grade. The General pinned the medal on Virginia's hospital gown and once again snapped off a salute. Virginia saluted back with a smile and said, 'Dankeshon'. The hospital staff applauded.

"I'll be dipped in hog shit," said Virginia admiring her award. "This is pretty big in your country, isn't it Fritz?"

"Huge. Hitler has one."

"I wonder how my Colonel would feel if he knew...oh screw him, I got a medal. I actually feel much better."

After every body cleared out of her room, the orderly brought Virginia her chocolate ice cream.

CHAPTER 40

VIRGINIA, SUPERSTAR

Virginia instantly went from a person of suspicion to a celebrity. The next day she needed to get up and move about. The girl managed to dress even though her head was still swimming from the hammer blow. She slipped into her uniform and then pinned the iron cross to the jacket along with the other citations on her uniform. Instead of someone yammering at Virginia for being out of the room, the girl was welcomed with smiles from the hospital staff and other patients. People approached her and shook her hand, patted her on the back and call her 'Lieutenant'. A German soldier passed her in the foyer leading outside and saluted, Virginia smiled and saluted back.

Virginia went and sat in a gazebo in the back of the hospital by a small pond by herself. It was a beautiful summer day…not a cloud or a bomber in the azure sky. Being a navigator and knowing exactly where she was in Germany, she was sure the American fleets of B-17 would not pass over this town at all. She was in the village of Laupheim. The town would not be bombed even though its train station was a minor hub for troop movements. The station was just not very important and the town itself was well protected by the natural surrounding terrain.

There was a German magazine in the hospital waiting room. Virginia didn't think anyone would mind if she took it out on the patio. She was sitting in the gazebo leafing through the pages of the periodical when her train of thought was derailed by a pretty German girl.

"May I join you Lieutenant?" the girl asked. She was not too tall, pretty, about 30ish, wrapped in a hospital bathrobe and her nose was heavily bandaged.

"Ya," said Virginia. "I guess so."

"Sure is a beautiful day, isn't it?" said the German.

"Ya, it sure is. Entschuldigen sie bitte," said Virginia in fine German, "what happened to your nose?"

"Oh, you noticed," said the lady, "crashed my plane on take off about two months ago. I was in the area doing an appearance for Goebbels and my nose began to ache so I stopped in here to have it looked at. A good thing too, an infection formed around the stitches. I can leave tomorrow morning. I heard about you and what you did Lieutenant, thank you."

"Nix zu danken," said Virginia in proper German.

The lady chuckled, "You speak sau gute Deutsche!"

"I just know a few words," said Virginia with a smile. "I'm Virginia White. What's your name?"

"Hanna Reitsch." Virginia's jaw dropped as she slide away from Ms. Reitsch on the bench. "Miss White, what is wrong? You look like you have seen a ghost!"

"I know who you are," said Virginia.

"Who am I, Lieutenant?"

"Der Fuehrer's go-to test pilot."

Hanna laughed, "You are right, hard to believe an American girl knows about me. But here you are. Virginia, I promise no talking about planes and the war. We can talk as two ladies from different countries."

"Can you do that, Hanna?"

"Promise!"

"Ok," agreed Virginia relaxing some around the famous German aviatrix. "Just tell me one thing."

"All right, one thing."

"What's it like to fly at 600 miles per hour?"

"How did you hear about that? That was supposed to be top secret. Verdammt you Amies are good. No matter…it was 663 mph."

"Wow Hanna, that's really flyin'. That has got to be…really swell!"

"It is not much different from flying at 300 mph. The clouds fly by faster and the horizon changes quickly. If anything should happen to cross my path, there is no time to move out of the way. The rocket engine is quiet compared to the gas engines. That's the true difference. It's like soaring without wings."

"Do you think jet engines will ever catch on?"

"Only on military aircraft. All others will remain the same."

The two ladies did not mention airplanes at all after that. Virginia told Hanna about Canton, Ohio and Hanna spoke about her father and three sisters. They only talked for an hour before Hanna was summoned to go inside.

"It was nice to meet you Virginia. I will need a friend in America when we conquer New York City," said Hanna with a smile.

"Nice to meet you too, I'll see you in Berlin, Hanna," retorted Virginia, with a sheepish grin and a small wave.

While the ladies were talking, they were interrupted by people greeting either Virginia or Hanna. Some gave Virginia chocolate bars which she smuggled back to her room and shared with her roommates.

¥

Just as a note from Linda had instructed, the next day Virginia was seated in front of the hospital waiting for her American friend's arrival. She saw Linda's big black boat (the Mercedes is black) arrive long before it pulled up to the door. Virginia hopped into the passenger seat.

After salutations, Virginia told Linda about meeting Hanna Reitsch and how they chatted for a while. Also, she spoke of the affection the hospital staff bestowed on her.

Linda drove off onto the paved road leaving the hospital, "What did you think of Reitsch?" she asked.

"She was very pleasant. Missing her nose but pleasant," said Virginia.

"She didn't try and pump you for information like those people do?"

"No Linda, she didn't. If anything, she divulged secrets of the Me-163. Why do you ask?"

"I don't like her. Fritz does not like her. Most of Europe does not like her. She's Hitler's little girl. The Nazis like her."

"I don't understand, we spoke of our families, Linda."

"Well, maybe she liked you," said Linda.

"Stranger things have happened…can't think of any right now."

"Neither can I," said the colored girl after a short uneasy pause.

They drove a while in silence. "Where are we going." asked Virginia. "Let me guess. We are going to do something you have always wanted to do but have not taken the time to do it."

"For a child you sure can be smart sometime. Have you ever been horseback riding?"

"No…but I've always wanted to go and try it."

"Me too!!"

While on the short drive to another vast estate on the edge of town, the conversation flowed from the US, family, to Fritz's work which Linda was not permitted to say much about. The two ladies seemed to always have something to talk about. They pulled onto the property and right up to the stables where a boy was waiting for them.

"Lieutenant," said the stable boy with a salute.

Virginia smiled and saluted back. "You're kidding me, Linda. This boy has heard about me?"

"Everyone has heard about you, Virginia. It's a small, close knit community. "

"I'll be dipped in shit," said Virginia.

Two well-tempered ponies were chosen for them. The stable boy saddled them up, the ladies mounted their steeds and ambled down a bridle trail. "You have become awfully quiet all of a sudden," commented Linda. "What's wrong, girl?"

"I'm not at all sure. I'm an American aviator. I bomb these people, that's what I do, that's what I've been trained to do and…I like doing it. Now look! I'm a German national hero for what? Just for saving that girl's life?"

"Virginia, when you did that quick surgery on that girl, did you see an American or a German or an Italian?"

"No, I saw a girl in trouble. I didn't think."

"You didn't think, you acted and saved a life. And what was your reward?"

Virginia thought for a moment, "A massive headache!"

"A massive headache. That is not the German way. They have to make amends. They don't see an American, they see someone who acted and save a life. Heroically. We need heroes today. You are one."

"Fine, but I'm not going to get used to it."

"But you are wearing your medal on your jacket…nice touch by the way."

"Are you kidding, it's an Iron Cross. I'll never get an honor like this at home." They both laughed.

The duo rode in silence for a while longer. "I'm not sure I should tell you this," said Linda. "Fritz is trying to get you repatriated."

"Re what?"

"Sent home."

A chill swept down Virginia's back but she didn't say anything.

"What's wrong? Don't you want to go home?"

"Ya, sure, I guess," said Virginia. *'What a perfect way to end a wonderful day'*, thought Virginia.

There was not much more to talk about as they surrendered their mounts to the awaiting stable boy, climbed into Linda's car that was as big as a whale, and headed back to the hospital.

CHAPTER 41

VIRGINIA IS A PRISONER...AGAIN

Everyone has one of those days. Things appear to be coming together before the other shoe falls. One must always be on the look out for that other shoe.

Virginia contemplated going home and began to become comfortable with the idea of seeing her mother and father instead of dying alone in Germany. She was beginning to sense her blood disease taking its toll on her body though she did not mention it.

When the ladies arrived at the hospital, they were met by Major Strasser. "It is about time you bring this prisoner back here, Lady Augustus. You have kept me waiting."

"Major Strasser, why would a pig like you be waiting for Lady Augustus?" demanded Linda.

"I am taking the American flyer."

"I think not!!"

"This is Gestapo business and none of yours."

"Maybe you should speak to my husband about your issues," replied Linda ever defiant to the Gestapo.

"In due time. You, American, get yourself on this truck right now," ordered the Major.

"WHAT?" protested Virginia.

"You heard me. Get on the truck or I'll have you shot." Virginia froze and looked over to Linda. "NOW!" growled Strasser.

"What do you want with Lieutenant White?" demanded Linda.

"She is going to be relocated where she can serve the Reich."

"Relocated? You can't just relocate her like that, she's a war hero."

"She is a prisoner-of-war of Germany. She will do as we want. You are trying my patience, Lady Augustus."

Linda shrugged her shoulders and shook her head. "Captain Augustus will hear about this, Major."

"He already has," he said shoving Virginia toward the truck. "And you had best stop interfering with Gestapo business or there will be two American women on this truck."

"Linda?" said Virginia.

Linda could see the fear and angst in the young American girl's eyes. "You better do as he says for now, Virginia. I'll find Fritz and clear this all up."

Linda urgently rushed off in her Mercedes to inform Fritz of what was happening. Virginia climbed in the back of the truck and joined two American soldiers already seated on the hard wooden benches. She felt like crying but that would not be very heroic so she sat quietly pulling her knees up to her chest.

¥

Linda rushed home to find Captain Fritz seated in a padded chair on the large patio behind the house sipping some straight 12 year old scotch. "Fritz, what are you doing? You never drink during the day and scotch? What the hell is going on?"

"Linda our world is coming to end!"

"Fritz, Major Strasser just drove off with Virginia in a truck!"

"I know, Linda," said Fritz calmly.

"You know?? And you are just going to sit there drinking scotch?"

"We are out of rum."

"Aren't you going to do something about Virginia and Major Strasser and all?"

"No. I can't."

"You can! You are an Augustus!! Your grandfather is Wilhelm the Second!! People listen to you!!'

"Linda, our world has come under siege. Germany will be destroyed not in months but in weeks. The Americans have crossed the Rhine, a General Paton has crossed at Oppenheim. They are rapidly approaching Berlin from the west and our depleted army can not stop them. Then we have the Russians advancing from the east. After Germany falls, there will be no place for the royal family. We will be blamed for all this."

"What about Virginia, can't we save her from what the Gestapo wants to do to her?"

"Virginia and her confederates are going to Frankfurt where they will be used as a human shield next to a chemical warfare research facility. The High Command feels that the Americans will not bomb the facility less they kill their own people. She will be one of 148 POW's housed there. There will be several women there with her."

"And there is not a thing you can do?" asked Linda.

"These are desperate times. I could be shot as a traitor if I make too much noise. Don't worry, she should be safe."

For some reason Linda could not agree with the Captain.

¥

Virginia climbed down out of the truck at her new home. So not to lose her medal, she quickly removed her Iron Cross and slipped it into her pocket. Once up on the third floor of a building in the center of town, a uniformed German showed Virginia to her room.

It actually had all the comforts of a hotel room in Cleveland. A single bed with a real mattress not a lumpy cloth bag filled with straw. There was a writing desk in front of a large sash window that really opened. She had her own bathroom with a tub and a shower with hot running water and a mirror above a sink with running water. She stood by the window smiling, happy with her new surroundings. "What are these Krauts up to?" she said aloud.

"We will find out soon enough," said a colonel in his British accent. "You find you accommodations suitable Lieutenant?"

"Yes, quaint but suitable," said Virginia in a poor British accent.

"I'm Colonel Barnes, senior POW officer. Here is a Red Cross package. Sorry we don't have any female packages so you will have to make do."

"Thaaaaaank yoooou Coooolonel Barnes."

"Have you gone daft, Lieutenant? Why are you talking like that?"

"I wasn't sure you spoke American or not."

CHAPTER 42

LIFE IS BORING

Once again life in a POW camp is dull at best. Virginia did learn that the language she speaks is not American but English and that English, with the exception of a few variations, is shared with several countries around the world. That was enlightening. *'That is why we study English in school not American,'* she thought to herself, *'Now I got it.'*

In the camp there were six other women all housed on the third floor. They were all nurses captured by the Germans. Four were American and two were British however that did not matter. The women all hung together doing sewing activities and telling stories of their adventures in Europe as well as back home. They had to be careful not to divulge any secrets to the Germans. Virginia hated sewing and usually sat quietly listening, seldom commenting. Life in the dorm was one long continuous grind.

The dormitory wasn't the same as her other camp. It was less lively and more depressing. Virginia had free rein of the building. She was permitted to leave her room, go outside and talk with the Germans. She met a few of the German women working in the lab next door while they were outside taking a smoking break. They were severely chastised by the Gestapo upon returning to their work. Then there was one particular German guard who took a liking to the American. He was very young, only a year older then Virginia. The Gestapo didn't seem to bother with his chatting with Virginia. He brought Virginia German chocolate and German wines. Virginia knew she should not accept the gifts but she felt it was alright as long as she shared with the other girls. More than a few times the couple sat, talked and actually laughed in Virginia's broken Deutsch and the German's broken English. The German's name was Wolfgang. That name made Virginia laugh. She thought it was a funny name. *'Who the hell names their kid Wolfgang?'* she rambled in her head, *'Here wolfy. In Ohio, that would bring on a pack of killer coyotes. That is as bad as Duane or Dwayne. D...wayne. I knew a kid name D...wayne in school,'* she continued to maul in her mind. *'No one liked him...his mother made him take accordion lessons...his mother hated D...wayne too.'* Wolfgang was a true Aryan. Tall with blonde hair, blue eyes, a square chin and lots of muscles.

Virginia was slipping into an ever darker pit of despair. She missed Fritz, Linda and the kids. She wondered how they were doing and then she wondered if they forgot about her. She kept her German medal in a hidden pocket inside her pocket. One of the British girls sewed it for her. The Iron Cross was well hidden and easily over looked each time she is searched by the goons (guards).

Then, in addition to her gloom, her blood illness was getting the better of her though she did not mention it to anyone. On one particular gloomy rainy German day, Virginia chose to stay in bed not even coming down for dinner...the worst thing she could do in her condition. Fortunately, one of the British girls, being a nurse and all, noticed her behavior and smuggled Virginia some dinner to her room. The Brit had to force the American to eat…something the English nurse was used to doing.

Finally, Virginia's love interest informed her that a visitor was on his way upstairs. *'Fritz,'* Virginia thought to herself. *'Who else could it be? My dad certainly isn't coming from Ohio.'* Sure enough Fritz stepped into the long hall opposite Virginia smiling at her.

"Fritz!!" shouted the American girl, "Fritz, I'm here!"

Fritz was half way down the hall when there was a loud and defending blast. Then, as if in slow motion, a fire ball engulfed the German Captain with arms and legs being flung in all directions. All this was quickly followed by a shock wave that lifted Virginia off her feet and dropped her onto the floor crumbling beneath her. The collapsing building began to disintegrate around her. She could hear people screaming but there was not a thing she could do to help them…it all seemed to be a bad dream.

After Virginia landed, she could not move. She felt cold and numb. The girl managed to lift her head and could see a broken pipe sticking out of her abdomen. *'At least it's something different,'* she chuckled before passing out.

CHAPTER 43

BRITISH PINPOINT BOMBING

On October 31, 1944, the Royal Air Force made a pin point bombing raid on the Gestapo Headquarters at the University of Aarhus in Aarhus, Denmark.

The Gestapo was making life very difficult for the Danish underground on the Jutland Peninsula. To add to their problems, a British agent was captured by the Gestapo and while being 'interrogated', he divulged information about the network of the resistance in the area. Needless to say, the Gestapo rounded up 145 people crippling the underground efforts. A telegram was sent to London requesting the RAF to bomb the Gestapo headquarters at Aarhus University.

The RAF was quick to draw up a plan. The target was especially difficult to bomb because there were two hospitals one on each side the targeted dormitories, so precision was mandatory. A 1:1 scale chalk outline of the area was made for the pilots to practice making bombing runs.

The plan was to use 25 De Havilland Mosquito fighter bombers in four waves. The first two waves would use regular one ton bombs to open the target while the next two would use incendiary bombs for total devastation. The attack would be between 11:30 and noon while the building occupants go to lunch at the dormitories.

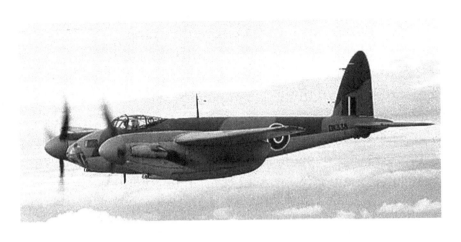

De Havilland Mosquito (25)

The very successful Mosquito was designed as a high speed bomber. It was 40 feet long with a 54 foot wing span. By 1944, the plane had two 1710 hp Merlin 76 engines propelling the Mosquito 425 MPH. In addition, it usually had four 20 mm cannons and four 30 caliber machine guns in the nose.

On October 31st, all went well. The 25 Mosquitoes were supported by eight P-51 Mustangs flown by the 315th, a Polish squadron. The 315th broke off from the group upon entering the airspace to draw German fighters off the Bombers. Each wave was successful and all returned to base except one Mosquito that was damaged by ground fire and landed in Sweden where the crew was interned until the end of the war.

The British destroyed the dorms with limited damage to the surrounding area. The Gestapo lost 39 agents and 20 Weremacht soldiers were killed. The Danes had a dozen fatalities.

¥

After numerous requests from the Danish underground, The British RAF opted to carry out 'Operation Carthage'. 'Operation Carthage' was the battle plan to bomb the Gestapo Headquarters in Copenhagen, Denmark. The headquarters were housed in a large six story building with three wings in the dead center of Copenhagen. It was used to house dossiers and to torture Danish citizens during 'interrogations'.

The British planned to fly in 20 De Havilland mosquito fighter bombers to blast the Gestapo's building with pinpoint accuracy so to limit collateral damage to the neighboring populace. The Mosquito was the British workhorse and the go-to aircraft for such operations.

The British strategy was to attack in three waves of six Mosquitoes. Supporting the bombers were 30 North American P-51 Mustang fighter planes. The British built a scaled mock up of Copenhagen to prepare the pilots for the attack.

On March 21, 1945, the first wave approached at roof top level. One of the Mosquitoes clipped its wing on a building and crashed into the Roman Catholic boarding school named Jeanne d' Arc and burst into flames. A few of the pilots from the second and third wave thought the burning school was the target and proceeded to bomb the school into rubble. 86 children and 18 adults, mostly nuns, were killed. The remaining Mosquitoes were very successful at dropping their bombs on the Gestapo's building with little damage to the surrounding area. The entire west wing of the building was reduced to ground level. The rest of the six story building was burning from end to end. The Gestapo's attempt to defeat the Danish resistance was finished. In addition, 55 Gestapo agents were killed along with 47 Danish employees who had it coming.

The British lost six planes and suffered nine deaths. Plus the 86 school children. The operation was considered a great victory even though the war ended one month later.

¥

After the highly successful British bombing mission in Aarhus, The Americans flew their own version of pinpoint precision bombing. On March 31st, 1944, they outlined a plan to bomb the building housing the chemical research facility in Frankfurt, Germany, without harming the POWs in the dormitory next door.

The American plan was similar to the British with the exception that the Americans planned on flying in a sole B-25 loaded with a single one ton block buster. The pilot was also the navigator and spotter for the bombardier. The plan was for the pilot to find the building, notify the bombardier, and then drop the bomb down its chimney.

Colonel Barry Balder was, well, a poor excuse for a pilot. The only reason Balder was promoted to Colonel was because his superiors advanced him so he would be moved out of their department. He received his pilot's license at the age of 17 and had a brilliant flying career over France in WW1 at 20. Since then, he failed to evolve as a pilot. When the Army introduced new flying techniques such as tight flying formations and new maneuvers, Balder never took the time to learn them. He became an annoyance continuing to believe he was competent and bored good pilots with tales of the first war.

Balder did go on to train for the pinpoint bombing mission. He was a perfect candidate, a lone pilot, not beholden to a squadron. After that mission, he would retire a full bird Colonel. Balder did well while training for the mission and showed promise of successfully flying the sensitive mission.

Barry Balder scored well in the practice missions at the airbase and was selected for the job. A scale mock-up of the town was made so he would recognize landmarks have no trouble finding the buildings. Everything seemed to be in order for the Americans.

So on April 2nd, 1944, Balder and his bombardier took off from their airbase in France for the short flight to Frankfurt. After they entered the skies over Frankfurt, Balder dropped to 500 feet and immediately became confused. Later he would viciously complain that the church spiral was not in the same place as the mock-up.

Balder made a second pass over the town still unmolested by German fighters. On the second pass, he was certain he had the right building and radioed the position to the bombardier. The plane passed over the building and the bomb dropped blowing up Virginia White's POW barracks.

Colonel Barry Balder committed suicide a month later.

CHAPTER 44

TIME TO GO HOME

The Germans were quick to come to the POW's rescue. Virginia was easily spotted lying on the top of a heap of bricks. The Germans gingerly lifted her straight up off the busted pipe opening the otherwise sealed wound in the girl's side allowing a river of blood to cascade onto the broken bricks. There was little to do except rush Virginia to a stretcher where an awaiting medic ripped open her uniform, turned the girl on her side, and then pressed a gauze pad on the entrance and exit wounds.

Virginia quietly murmured when she and the medic were loaded into the ambulance, dripping blood through the stretcher. With red lights flashing they rushed the few blocks to the hospital. "Fritz, Fritz, where is Fritz?" demanded Virginia. The medic did not understand. At the scene of the bombing, no other ambulances were necessary.

The Germans are not known for wasting time. Once Virginia was inside the big double hospital doors, she was stripped and prepped for emergency surgery. Her bloody uniform was tossed onto the floor were a young female orderly stuffed it into a burlap sack.

Once the bandages were removed her blood flowed like Niagara Falls onto the operating table and then the floor. The doctors finally managed to stop the bleeding but Virginia was white as a ghost due to blood loss. Her pulse was weak and her blood pressure was inhumanly low. Major Straus said to let her die but that was not the German doctor's way. A transfusion of type A+ was pumped into the American girl. Once she was stabilized, the doctors could focus on her wounds.

During the operation, Virginia lost another river of blood. Her spleen was removed, she was stitched up, 225 sutures, and another transfusion of A+ blood was pumped into the American girl by the Germans. After all their efforts, all the doctors could do was wait. A young female orderly was posted by her bed that night to monitor her progress until morning.

At around 3 am, three days later, Virginia woke. It was April 1 1945, 10 days before her 18th birthday and her being old enough to join the Army. After opening her eyes Virginia's mind cleared. She looked under her covers to see herself once again wrapped in bandages. "Now what?" she said aloud.

"Now what? You get to go home!" said a young smiling American Army nurse.

"Who are you?" asked Virginia politely.

"I'm Toni, your nurse. I'm very glad to see you awake, Virginia. The Germans did a wonderful job patching you up."

"Where are we…home?'

"No, not yet. The 5th Infantry took Frankfurt about three days ago. We found you in their hospital. A German nurse gave me this thing to give to you." Toni handed Virginia her Iron Cross. "The German said you would want it."

Virginia smiled and closed her fist around her medal. "Thanks…Toni."

"Can I get you anything?"
"Sure, a cheese burger and fries."
"I'll see what I can do for a war hero."

¥

"For me, the war ended at the end of April 30, 1945, when that crazy bastard shot himself," said Mrs. Morgenstern. "The American doctors said I was in perfect health. The Germans unknowingly cured my blood disease with the blood transfusions. My blood type is no longer AB negative but A positive. The only A+ I ever got. The virus I carried was gone too. It must not have survived the loss of my own blood. The plague brought upon the German people also ran itself out. It appears that the virus had a short life span.

"I stayed in Germany until the middle of June. Germany is a beautiful country when no one is trying to kill you. After the war, the German people were friendly and cordial to the Americans. I guess they were happy to still be alive after seeing so many of their friends and family being blown to bits.

"In June, I caught a hop to England. It was a B-25. Instead of taking a seat at the navigator's table, I sat in the bombardier's place so I could look out the Plexiglas bubble. I wanted to be sure we were landing in England. I smiled when I saw the white cliffs of Dover. It was a beautiful sight.

"Things went well in England. Upon arrival, I was ordered to Hardwick by General George Daniels. There, in front of the entire base personnel, I was presented the 'Medal of Honor' and then promoted to Captain. Imagine 18 years old and a Captain in the Army.

"I stayed in Hardwick for another year before my hitch was up. There was a demand for experienced navigators to teach the basics to new enlistees. I could have reenlisted but the modern techniques made my talents obsolete especially with the new jet fighters. Besides, it was time to go home.

"I could have taken a military flight from England to the US but I had plenty of money so I opted to buy a ticket on Eastern Airlines. The commercial flights were much more comfortable than a military plane being bounced around crammed in the back with the rest of the cargo. While I was at the ticket counter at Heathrow Airport near London booking my flight, an employee of Eastern came over from two counters down. He said my money was no good and gave me my ticket at no charge. I was still wearing my American Captain's dress uniform. It was the only clothes I had. The British ticket agent snapped off a salute which I returned in a proper fashion.

"The flight, on board a commercial Douglas DC-3, was pleasant. People bought me drinks…they didn't ask how old I was. I spoke with a big Marine who was going home too, Milwaukee, Wisconsin. A Packers fan. We landed at the Eastern hub in New York City where there was a five hour lay over before my flight to Canton, Ohio.

"The Marine had spent some time in New York so he knew his way around the city. He asked me to go to the city with him and take in all the sights. He promised to have us back at the airport before my plane took off. It was probably the alcohol talking but I was quick to agree. I found a pay phone (that is a public phone that people could use by putting money in) at the airport and called city hall in Canton so they could tell my parents when I would be arriving at the NEW airport outside of Canton. We didn't have a phone at my house in Canton so the people at the city hall would send a car to my house to convey the message…I hoped.

"What a wonderful time. Our uniforms got us into the museums for free. We lunched in Central Park and saw the Empire State Building. We were able to go to the observation deck on the 102nd floor even though repairs were still being made from when, of all planes, a B-25 bomber hit the building at the 79th floor in the fog in July the previous year. We had lunch in Little Italy. We ate pizza at a quaint little pizzeria called Amalfi's. The owner brought us his best Chianti and again there was no charge but I gave our waitress a 5 spot.

"My plane was in its final boarding when my bud and I returned to the airport. I kissed the big guy good bye and then scrambled up the stairs onto the plane and into my seat. The flight to Canton was only a little over an hour long. We would be landing at brand new airport called 'Akron-Canton-Mansfield Airport'. My flight was one of the first passenger flights to land there even though the airport was still not open to commercial flights.

"I feel asleep on the plane so it was very short. A stewardess woke me in time to look out my window to see the airport. I wasn't sure the sleep was out of my eyes because I could not believe what I saw. There were several hundred people gathered along the tarmac and the gate. I thought Bob Hope or Edward G. Robinson was on the plane. I asked the stewardess who was so important on the plane. She said no one special except a war hero. Well that explained it. There had to be someone of great importance for that many people to show up at a new airport.

"Upon arrival, I dug in my knap sack for the case that held my 'Medal of Honor'. After slipping it over my head, I adjusted my cap and pinned my Iron Cross under my other citations. My nerves were on edge as I queued up with the other passengers to exit the plane. I had not seen or heard from my mom and dad in four years. Why would they even show up at the airport? Why would anyone show up? I hoped there was a bus to take me home.

"When I stepped out of the plane, on the top of the stair case, the crowd of hundreds erupted in cheers. I froze as they yelled my name and waved American flags. 'Vir-gin-ia, Vir-gin-ia, Vir-gin-ia.' The great Army Captain, bomber girl, American hero, turned around and tried to hide back on the plane but the two stewardesses wouldn't have it and they wrestled me back on the stairs. I smiled, almost in tears and waved back to people I knew. Childhood friends, classmates, my two sisters and my mom and dad. It appeared that my father had a telephone installed at our house in Canton and he received a phone call from a General Daniels in Washington.

"I walked down the stairs with my head held high periodically waving to the folks gathered there. At the bottom of the stairs, I was ambushed by none other than my dad. He hugged so hard I couldn't breath. Then he kissed me on both my cheeks. My dad never hugged me before."

Tears begin to erupt from the old woman's eyes. She then opened a draw in an old marred wooden table in the atrium and pulled out a small case. After opening the case, the American Bomber Girl produced a 'Medal of Honor'.

"Mom," said Jennifer, "Why? Why haven't you told me this before?"

"It was top secret, Jennifer," I interjected, "They swore to take the story of the American Bomber Girls to their grave."

Ms. Morgenstern was fighting back the tears. "When I look at this medal, I ask myself how did I do it. I should have thrown it away decades ago. It is nothing more than a remembrance. It reminds me of the girls I flew with. Jennifer, Honey, Sandy, Teresa and of course Julie. I also remember seeing Fritz being blown apart. I see it just like it happened yesterday."

Ms Morgenstern grew quiet. I didn't say anything and neither did Jennifer. "GET OUT, MR. MUNTEAN!"

"Mom," said Jennifer quietly.

"Get out now, or I'll call the police."

"As you wish, Ms. Morgenstern."

Jennifer and I left Ms. Morgenstern alone in the atrium amongst her flowers. The old woman's shoulders sagged. I saw her attempt to take a deep breath. "I'm sorry Bill," said Jennifer. "She gets this way once in a while. I never knew why…until now."

"You have nothing to apologize for Jennifer. I did not mean to upset your mother."

"Are you going to write the story?" asked Jennifer.

"It is a story that must be told. Your mother and her friends did a great service to the US at a time they were needed the most. They were, are heroes. The American people need to know how the sacrifice of a small group of women affected the outcome of the war. And besides, if I don't write the story, there will be others here wanting to interview your mother. Someone else will write it."

Jennifer opened the door out to my car. "I look forward to reading it," she said with a smile.

"I'll send you an autographed copy. It was a pleasure to meet you Jennifer."

FINI

The author, Bill, on his 50 cal.

Attributes for the photos that are not Public Domain:

(1) Lukas skywalker - Own work
https://en.wikipedia.org/wiki/North_American_B-25_Mitchell#/media/File:North_American_B-25_Mitchell_G%C3%B3raszka_2007.jpg

(2) This work is in the **public domain** in Turkey because it has been expropriated as national heritage or its copyright has expired. Article 27 of the Turkish copyright law states:
https://commons.wikimedia.org/wiki/File:Sabiha_gokcen2.jpg

(3) Foto: Collectie Rene Ros
https://www.google.com/search?q=Luftnachrichten-helferinnen&tbm=isch&tbo=u&source=univ&sa=X&ved=0ahUKEwi4l-ronJnZAhUDylMKHdY6AHIQsAQIKA&biw

(4) Bundesarchiv, Bild 183-B02092 / Schwahn / CC-BY-SA 3.0
https://da.wikipedia.org/wiki/Hanna_Reitsch#/media/File:Bundesarchiv_Bild_183-B02092,_Hanna_Reitsch.jpg

(5) Bundesarchiv_Bild_146-1972-058-62,_Raketenjäger_Me_163_A-V4.jpg
https://commons.wikimedia.org/wiki/File:Bundesarchiv_Bild_146-1972-058-62,_Raketenj%C3%A4ger_Me_163_A-V4.jpg

(6) ITAR-TASS (Federal State Unitary Enterprise wholly owned by Russian government)
https://commons.wikimedia.org/wiki/File:Marina_Raskova_portrait.png

(7) Original uploader was B. Huber at de.wikipedia
https://en.wikipedia.org/wiki/Messerschmitt_Bf_109#/media/File:Bf109V1Zeichnung2.jpg

(8) It is believed that the use of this image may qualify as **fair use** under the Copyright law of the United States
https://en.wikipedia.org/wiki/File:Litvyak,_Budanova_and_Kuznetsova.jpg

(9) Po=2 Bundesarchiv, Bild 169-0112 / CC-BY-SA 3.0
https://commons.wikimedia.org/wiki/File:Bundesarchiv_Bild_169-0112,_Russland,_erbeutetes_Flugzeug_Po-2.jpg

(10) Courtesy of image works
https://www.google.com/search?tbm=isch&q=Russian+public+domain+ww+2+photos&chips=q:russian+public+domain+ww+2+photos,online_chips:history

(11) Bundesarchiv, Bild 101I-345-0780-14A / Speck / CC-BY-SA 3.0
https://commons.wikimedia.org/wiki/File:Bundesarchiv_Bild_101I-345-0780-14A,_Frankreich,_abgest%C3%BCrztes_Flugzeug.jpg

(12) This work is in the **public domain** in its country of origin and other countries and areas where the copyright term is the author's **life plus 70 years or less**.

{{PD-US-not renewed}} – published and copyrighted in the United States between 1923 and 1963, with its copyright not renewed

(13) *This photograph is in the **public domain** in Finland, because either a period of 50 years has elapsed from the year of creation or the photograph was first published before 1966.*

(14) Source War Thunder

https://forum.warthunder.com/index.php?/topic/171506-escadrila-alb%C4%83-romanian-women-in-skies-during-wwii/

(15) This work is in the **public domain** in its country of origin and other countries and areas where the copyright term is the author's **life plus 70 years or less.**

https://commons.wikimedia.org/wiki/File:Mariana_Dragescu_preTakeOff_casualty.jpg

(16) *This work created by the United Kingdom Government is in the **public domain**.*
https://commons.wikimedia.org/wiki/File:Walker_Spitfire.jpg

(17) Daily Mail.com
http://www.dailymail.co.uk/femail/article-3194754/The-female-Guns-World-War-II-Inside-RAF-s-woman-ferry-squadron-rubbed-shoulders-men-flew-Spitfires.html

(18) This file is a Ukrainian or Ukrainian SSR work and it is presently in the public domain *in Ukraine*, because it was published before January 1, 1951, *and* the creator (if known) died before that date

https://commons.wikimedia.org/wiki/File:Pavlichenko_LM.jpg

(19) **Bundesarchiv, Bild 101I-656-6103-09 / Morocutti / CC-BY-SA 3.0**
https://commons.wikimedia.org/wiki/File:Bundesarchiv_Bild_101I-656-6103-09,_Reichsgebiet.-_Flak-Turm_mit_schwerer_Flak.jpg

(20) Ssaco Own work
https://commons.wikimedia.org/wiki/File:B-25H.jpg

(21) AElfwine at the French language Wikipedia
https://commons.wikimedia.org/wiki/File:Fus%C3%A9e_V2.jpg

(22)*This work created by the United Kingdom Government is in the **public domain**.*
https://commons.wikimedia.org/wiki/File:Fw_190A-3_JG_2_in_Britain_1942.jpg

(23) **Bundesarchiv, Bild 101I-377-2801-013 / Jakobsen [Jacobsen] / CC-BY-SA 3.0**
https://commons.wikimedia.org/wiki/File:Bundesarchiv_Bild_101I-377-2801-013,_Flugzeug_Messerschmitt_Me_110.jpg

(24) German Public Domain

(25) This Canadian work is in the public domain in Canada

https://commons.wikimedia.org/wiki/File:De_Havilland_DH-98_Mosquito_ExCC.jpg

(26) This image is in the **public domain** in Denmark because the Danish Consolidated Act on Copyright of 2010

https://commons.wikimedia.org/wiki/File:RAF_Attack_on_Aarhus_University_Gestapo_headquarters_31_October_1944_,_Langelandsgades_Kaserne.jpg